BUILDING IN PLACE

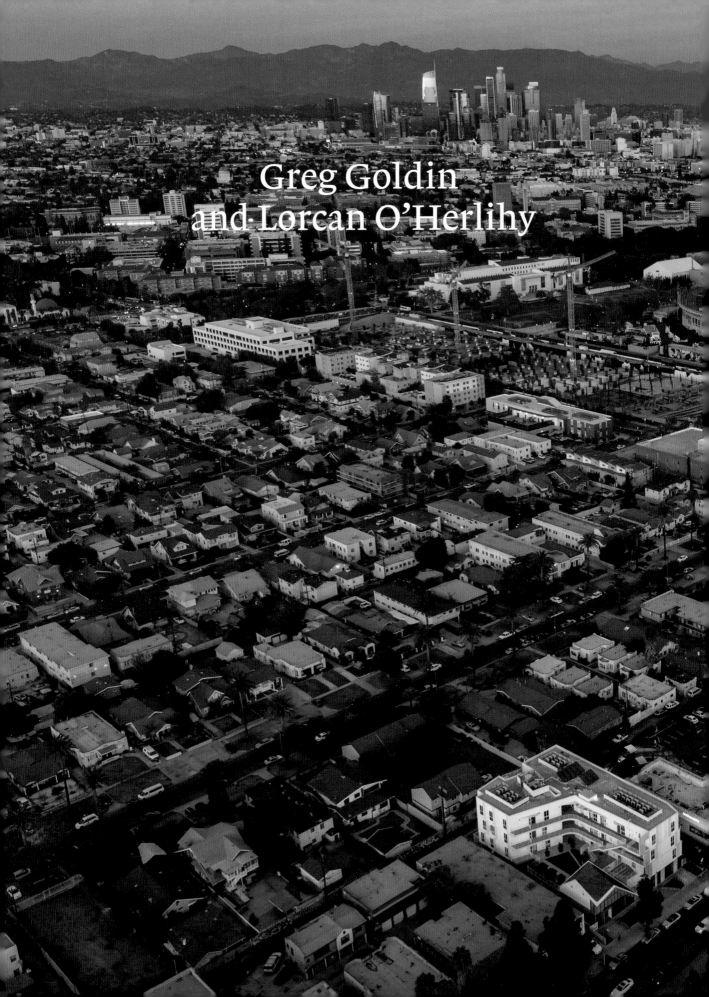

Greg Goldin
and Lorcan O'Herlihy

LORCAN O'HERLIHY ARCHITECTS

BUILDING IN PLACE

Architecture Rooted in Context and Social Equity

RIZZOLI
NEW YORK

CONTENTS

9
Acknowledgments

10
Introduction

14 CANYON5
Los Angeles, CA

30 MLK1101
SUPPORTIVE HOUSING
Los Angeles, CA

44 BRUSH PARK
Detroit, MI

64 UCSB SAN JOAQUIN
STUDENT HOUSING
Santa Barbara, CA

80 WILLOUGHBY 7917
West Hollywood, CA

96 CLOVERDALE 749
Los Angeles, CA

110 SL11024
Los Angeles, CA

126 SANDI SIMON CENTER FOR
DANCE AT CHAPMAN UNIVERSITY
Orange, CA

142 FORMOSA 1140
West Hollywood, CA

152 GRANVILLE 1500
AND WESTGATE 1515
Los Angeles, CA

172 OBAMA BUILDING
Detroit, MI

186 SOUTH EAST 8
Raleigh, NC

198 SYCAMORE 953
Los Angeles, CA

212 ISLA INTERSECTIONS
Los Angeles, CA

226 DILLON 617
Los Angeles, CA

238 SAN VICENTE 935
West Hollywood, CA

254
Project Credits

To my beloved wife, Leila,
whose love inspires me daily.

ACKNOWLEDGMENTS
Lorcan O'Herlihy

The ideas embedded in this book represent things that I have wanted to put into the pages of a book since the foundation of my practice. Even in my college thesis, "Towards New Models of Social Connectivity," the ideals that are highlighted in this book are present. It has been a great pleasure to work with Rizzoli on realizing this long-standing ideological thread in a publication. Of course, I would have not been able to put this book together without the tireless efforts of my collaborators, Greg Goldin, who wrote the book and tells the story of what I like to call "living histories" of LOHA's work, and Timothy O'Connell, whose photography tells the stories of the people and neighborhoods surrounding our projects, which I call "neighborhood portraits."

Many thanks to Lorraine Wild and Naveen Hattis of Green Dragon Office for their incredible work in designing such a beautiful book. We are honored to work with very talented and capable graphic designers.

This powerful combination, along with project photography by Paul Vu, Eric Staudenmaier, Iwan Baan, Lawrence Anderson, John Linden, Keith Isaacs, and Bruce Damonte, gives this book such a unique quality in the way it represents my practice's work.

This book would not have been possible without all of the dedicated work of everyone at LOHA, including our two directors, Ghazal Khezri and Brian Adolph, who played a crucial role in driving LOHA forward, and of our associates Abel Garcia, Geoffrey Sorrell, Kevin Murray, Jason King, Haylie Chan, Nicholas Muraglia, and all the wonderful colleagues past and present. Many thanks to Seymour Polatin, who worked closely with Greg and Timothy, conducting research, managed on-site photography and worked tirelessly to make this book happen.

To the team at Rizzoli, we are so lucky to work with like-minded editors who supported us at every turn to produce the best book possible.

To our clients, it is such a pleasure to work with committed colleagues who share our vision for social engagement and see the possibilities that architecture can bring to all.

INTRODUCTION

Building in Place, the title of the reflections on the works in this new volume, has more than a one intentional double entendre. Take the first word, building, which can be the verb, as in to construct an edifice, to fabricate from scratch, to raise something from the ground up. It also refers to the noun, as in a building, a structure. Place, too, has multiple meanings, as in to put something somewhere, such as to place an object on a table or a building on a plot of land. Then there's another meaning as in someplace, somewhere, a specific location, with the deeper, subtle connotation, implying a spot with a very specific history, culture, identity, appearance, tone, vibe, call it what you will, but alive with the beat of its own existence often too manifold to be expressed easily in words. Put the two together, and that is what we do. We build in place. When we're fortunate and successful, we manage to add our expression, in the form of a building, to the kinetic kaleidoscope of streets and sidewalks and storefronts and, of course, the people who make a place a place.

This doesn't happen by accident. Nor does it happen with unerring logic or surgical intention. Certainly, it doesn't occur by simply building isolated objects driven by formal polemics or a preconceived aesthetic. Our buildings are not arguments for an idea or a look or a solution to a social ill. Rather, I think of architecture as telling a story. It is about specific lives and specific places, the exact location where people work and play and carry out their daily routines, whether uplifting and inspiring or enervating and mind-numbing. The stories in this book are about redlining in south Los Angeles and the continuous renewal in the cultural and artistic melting pot of Silver Lake. They're about embracing the pessimism and economic struggles in Brush Park, in the collapsed ruins of Detroit. They're about implanting something brand new—housing for the unhoused—on a railway median, beneath one of the world's largest freeway overpasses, where there was no hope of life before. They're about the percolating waters of a timeless American Indian oasis hidden in the rush hour streets of a blithely unknowing metropolis. They are about a California seaside littoral of unrivaled splendor, buried yet reasserting itself as ancient nature speaks across time and generations. They are about listening quietly to a building across the street, as when we were inspired by the connection between nature and man-made shelter in Richard Neutra's Strathmore Apartments, to bring chartreuse and vivid whites and stepped volumes and deep voids to a steep slope that otherwise would have been molded into a blank stucco crate.

We embrace these stories and many others as assets and strengths, not constraints. In areas where there is tension and indifference on the streets we pause and listen and then challenge the unease and bring what is needed to build a sense of home or a sense of workplace, to uplift those who experience them. I'm convinced this gives our work consequence and gives back to the cities where we build.

In a sense, the present volume is a retrospective journey in which we invite you, the reader, along to see if we've succeeded in blurring the divisions between city and building. Have we found a way to unite street to site? Have we managed to keep alive those entwined economic and aesthetic forces that make cities robust? Have we been able to add a new language of architecture that doesn't blot out the old? Are we part of lifting the city up, or letting it down?

I ask these questions of myself by wandering back to the buildings we've built. Revisiting is a crucial part of our practice. Over the past thirty years we've come up with countless new designs and built many of them, but the act of revisiting is quieter, contemplative, introspective. What can a building tell us, five years, ten years, twenty years after its completion? Of course, my reexamination sits outside of the experience of the people who live in, work in, interact with, and walk by these projects daily. For them, these buildings make up a piece of their landscape. Perhaps they don't even notice them? Or they do, but because no one has interrogated them about their reactions, they've merely absorbed the buildings no differently than they would a tree or parked car. When I return to these buildings, I take the chance to engage the people who've formed relationships with our designs, who've spent more time with these projects than I possibly could. I like the interaction. I pose questions. I try to learn something about their lives, and why they chose to live in the buildings we've designed. What do they think of the way our buildings sit in the neighborhood? Do they like the dynamics of metalwork or the color scheme? How does it feel to step out your front door to the street or vice versa? In this way, the act of revisiting becomes a process of the new.

This also helps me begin to see things around the building. The curb, the gutter, street signs, passing cars, trees, the changing light, bursts of color, sounds, silences. Your senses begin to be engaged, and animated, by all those things you could not possibly have taken account of when designing. We do not design for context per se. Nor do we turn to the vernacular to influence our work. But I hope that over time, our buildings become part of the vernacular, that they are absorbed into their setting. They assume a life by standing in place. If we're lucky, this gives them a long life-span. Care flows from a sense that something belongs, and the transition from immediacy, newness, to memory. That's our goal—to become part of memory, the kind of memory one speaks of when talking about muscle memory. You don't have to think about it. It's just there, included in the warp and weft, part of the fabric. When a building disappears it truly becomes a landmark.

Much of our work has been in my hometown, Los Angeles. Los Angeles is a city that doesn't seem to make a lot of sense. Maybe it is for this reason that people frequently think it doesn't have much history. The truth is, as is almost always the case, the lack of understanding of the city's history leads to a lack of understanding of the city itself. The movie industry, which indirectly brought me here after my father moved us from Ireland, also contributes to misperceptions about the factors that shape the urban experience. No vision of a city could be more false, yet more believable, than the one spun by Tinseltown (although, nowadays, even Hollywood cannot put a glossy face on the housing crisis that has so profoundly afflicted Los Angeles). Conversely, Detroit—where a number of the projects in this book are located and where in recent years we've been working extensively—is a city that seemingly has a straightforward history of prosperity and decline, and has become shorthand for the collapse of the American manufacturing metropolis. The hardscrabble truth is too naked in Detroit to hide in a reassuring fairy tale.

Practicing in two single-industry-dominated towns, we take the responsibility of unpacking these environments and listening to lived experiences, through the locals, or through a process of uncovering when there are no more voices left. As architects, we have the rare opportunity to alter the city itself, to take genuine histories, build upon them, and redress the biases and myths that have shaped neighborhoods. Or confront inescapable truths with, I hope, care and optimism.

Working on this book has given me the chance to spend time with the works we've created over the years and reflect on their impact. We push for our designs to simultaneously recognize their surroundings and history while driving toward a larger public good. It is only through a comprehensive understanding of the inequalities that shape our cities that we can work to repair them. How can a privately owned apartment complex give back to a neighborhood? How can a desolate traffic median enrich a community? Why can't one building's courtyard also function as a public square for the entire block? These are the ostensibly impossible questions that we work with and hope to answer. These are the stories found in this book.

There is one story I left out. This may seem odd, since I would say it was probably one of, if not the defining moment of my early years in architecture. In 2003, I was hired to design an apartment complex next door to the Schindler House from 1922, truly the birthplace of modernist architecture in Los Angeles. The MAK Center, the Viennese foundation that then, as now, owned Schindler's pinwheel masterpiece of intersecting indoor and outdoor living spaces resting gently on the land, cried foul. Barely looking at my design, they proclaimed its forbidding weight, as they saw it, would bury Schindler's fragile redwood and concrete "paradise" in a dark crevasse. They convened an architectural competition, in effect, to derail my project. Suddenly, I found myself in a tempest, voice carried off by the gale of architects who'd blown into town to make grandiose pronouncements about a site they had never visited. This while the head of the MAK proclaimed: "the main task for architecture is, even as the dynamics of a city are changing … consider the site. You can't say it doesn't matter—and just build a building." He was right, but I never thought otherwise. I produced my original design: a composition of interlocking cubes, skinned in a variety of materials, spatially unimposing, respectful of the landmark next door, yet avowedly modern in its own right. Building next door to one of the world's greatest twentieth-century houses, amid a storm of controversy, imbued my work with an outlook I've held to this day: tread lightly, but never, ever fear to tread.

The handful of projects represented in this book reveal moments from my career, but whether they were built when I was establishing my practice, before or after that watershed moment, or are under construction as I write this now, each has a unique story to tell and is actively affecting its historical context. My mission for this book was to show what too often isn't seen in architecture—the moments of inspiration, the stories from neighbors, what I like to call living histories. This is because no building lives in isolation and architecture is best when it listens as much as it speaks.

Through research, writing, photography, and design, my collaborators and I have retraced my steps in the process of revisiting, meeting new people, hearing new stories, learning new histories. If you are familiar with my work, it is possible that you have seen some of these projects before, but I can assure you that you have not experienced them as they are presented in this book. It is a pleasure to be able to show these projects within the larger city and to represent the surrounding life.

In contrast to a catalogue raisonné or a manifesto, I see this book as a three-dimensional snapshot of our work, capturing the moment and place in time from which the projects emerged and, if we've done well, will thrive. History is not linear; neither is experience. Both are subjective. In this way, it is impossible to document architecture without trying to capture the conscious, human experience. To look at a building is to look through it and to recognize that there is no one, pure representation. It is through this fractured lens that the buildings look outward, and I hope this book reveals what it sees.

CANYON5

→ P. 255

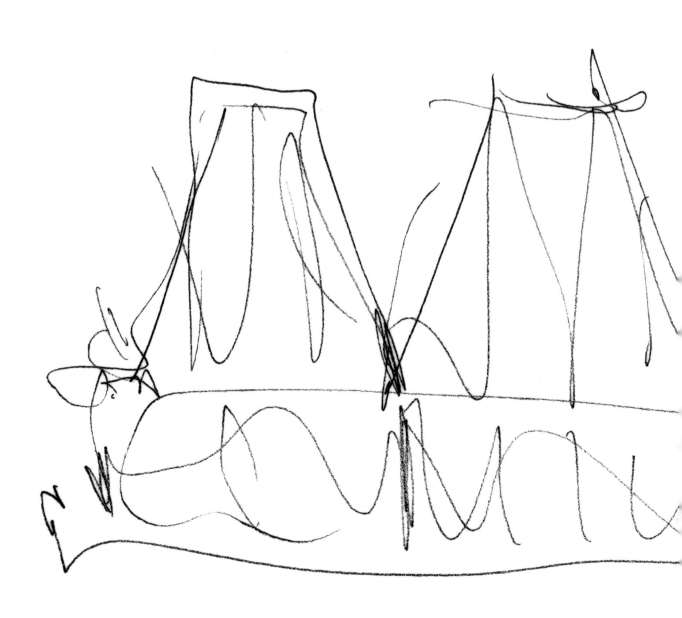

There always was, and still is, another Hollywood. The familiar Hollywood is the invented one, spun from tales of its own excesses, a state of mind more than a physical place, once described by the literary critic Alfred Kazin as "an industry commanding a town" with a "lurid reputation for opulence and the idiosyncrasy a special race of people permitted themselves." Novelists read into Hollywood the essence of the American identity: innocence soiled by cupidity, fraud gilded by relentless self-promotion, plunder disguised as charity. F. Scott Fitzgerald, in his posthumous and incomplete novel *The Last Tycoon* (1941), sketches the downfall of his committed producer, Monroe Stahr, who puts art above money; Sammy Glick, in Budd Schulberg's *What Makes Sammy Run?* (1941) is a ruthless schemer who'll stop at nothing in his climb to the top of the movie business; in Norman Mailer's *The Deer Park* (1955), Hollywood is a fraternity engaged day and night in depravity and debauchery; Maria Wyeth, Joan Didion's heroine in *Play It as It Lays* (1970), suffers a nervous breakdown in the maw of all that "degeneracy." But it was Nathanael West's *The Day of the Locust* (1939) that truly excoriated the Hollywood of the masses—the grifters, bookies, prostitutes, vacuous actresses and unemployed actors, and daydreamers—the throng whose love-hate of the glistening filmland idols ends in a climactic riot at "the world premiere of a new picture." West's Hollywood ends in bedlam. Amid the stars and searchlights, a crowd of thousands wait for the celebrities to arrive, tear into each other grabbing anything and anyone they can, and let loose a storm of violence.

West based his riot on a real riot that occurred on the night of May 18, 1927, at the grand opening of Grauman's Chinese Theatre on Hollywood Boulevard. Mayhem erupted among the 50,000 fans hoping to glimpse movie stars as they arrived for the premiere of Cecil B. DeMille's *The King of Kings*. The hungry, sometimes insatiable, crowds that gather in the footprinted forecourt of Grauman's keep the celebrity myths alive, but another building, tucked into a quiet residential part of Hollywood, actually embodied its real decadence. It was christened in 1929 as Château Elysée, a seven-story apartment house and hotel with turrets and cone-shaped roofs and Louis XIV interiors intended as a replica of a seventeenth-century Norman castle. That the structure borrowed from the architecture of France but bore no resemblance to its ostensible namesake, the original Palais de l'Elysée, one of the finest examples of French neoclassical architecture, was another proof that Hollywood was fiction, not fact. No matter. The entire beau monde congregated and fooled around there:

Curved exterior walls peel away from neighboring lots while tilted interior walls maintain privacy between units. Angled wall studs and panelized systems support the project's unique curved forms.

A-frame-shaped glazed façades gradually expand to maximize usable square footage on the interior.

Gloria Swanson and Bette Davis, Cary Grant and Katharine Hepburn, Carole Lombard, Ginger Rogers, Lillian Gish, George Gershwin, Edward G. Robinson, Clark Gable, Humphrey Bogart, Gracie Allen and George Burns. Edgar Rice Burroughs churned out volumes of Tarzan's adventures in room 408, and Errol Flynn went down to the garage to play poker with the chauffeurs. You could put your hands in the concrete prints on Hollywood Boulevard, but you weren't going to see the real goings-on unless you had entrée at the Château a mile and a half away, on Franklin Avenue.

Had you crossed the street and walked one block west, however, you'd have departed the licentious Hollywood and entered the other, a more sedate and modest one, founded in the late nineteenth century by Harvey and Daeida Wilcox as a utopian Christian farming village. The slopes above and below Franklin Avenue produced excellent lemons (hence Lemon Grove Avenue,

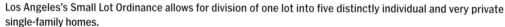

Los Angeles's Small Lot Ordinance allows for division of one lot into five distinctly individual and very private single-family homes.

Wood framing carries a sense of geometry inside the home.

Individual roof-decks provide outdoor space for each resident.

It's about clarity of the idea and less about formal polemics. It's more about seeing program as something that can be valuable to ideas while not getting overly consumed by that.

which cuts straight through the town), tangy oranges (used for orange soda, not fresh juice), and an impressive range of fruit from bananas to figs, apricots, avocados, dates, pineapples, and cherimoyas. One block west of the Château, Cheremoya Avenue and Cheremoya Avenue Elementary School (with four extant cherimoya trees in its yard), live on as misspelled reminders of the not-quite-forgotten agrarian past.

In 1911, another batch of high-minded settlers, the Theosophical Society, bought a large chunk of the Hastings Ranch in the hills below the present-day site of the Hollywood sign to farm and build its Krotona colony, a retreat where the vegetarian sect could meditate, practice their mix of mysticism and spiritualism, and map their goal of leading humanity toward brotherhood and unity. "We can make the spot a veritable Garden of Eden, because … the region we have chosen happens to be one of those rare spots that are absolutely frostless, and so we can raise anything," one of Krotona's founders said.

Springing up around these noble pursuits were streets filled with middle-class one- and two-story bungalows and Craftsman homes—solid, elegant, well made. The very opposite of the gaudy, ornate, faux-history-encrusted houses built at the behest of the *other* Hollywood. An idyllic quiescence has finally settled on these streets after more than one hundred years of habitation. The swirl and press of the nearby boulevards recedes beneath the trees and woodsy overhanging eaves. Residential Hollywood is of the city but not always totally steeped in the city.

Canyon5 shares this mature feeling of seclusion, the seclusion one meets when turning off a grand Parisian boulevard onto a tiny *rue*. The hubbub doesn't cease; it is subdued. The row of five houses, each with its distinctive hunchbacked, mansard-like walls—another signature French architectural style, made popular under the nineteenth-century emperor, Napoleon III—sits perpendicular to the street, raised above wood-clad garages facing a wide, open driveway. Set this way, the irregular forms compose a modern mews. Sedate, unimposing, an organic part of the living fabric of that other place also called Hollywood.

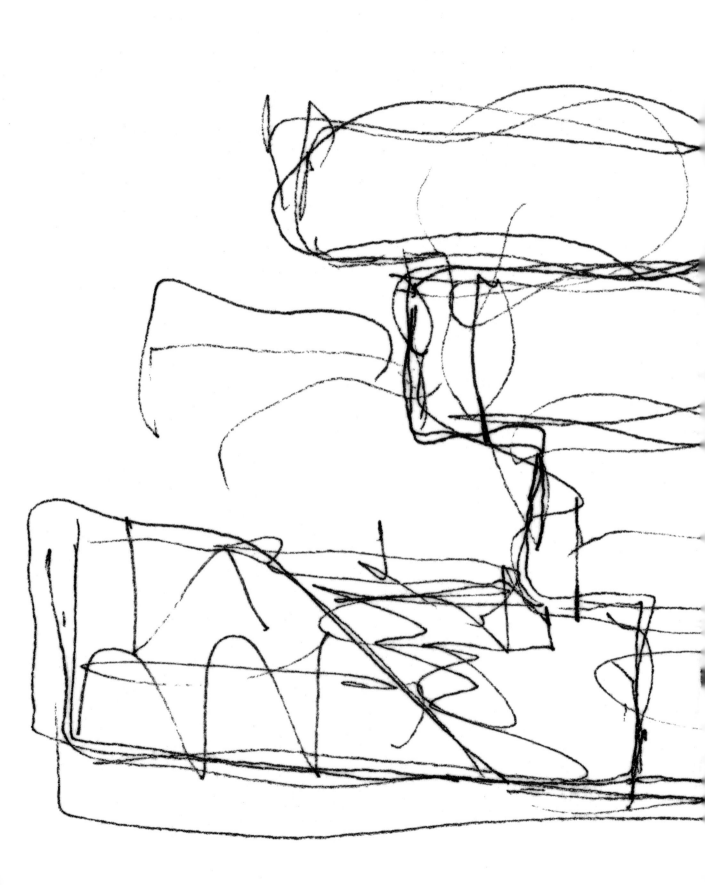

MLK1101 SUPPORTIVE HOUSING

→ P. 256

There is something about a bench-high, foot-and-a-half thick wall and an open space bounded by the weight of a building, like a canyon or a rock ledge, that invites sitting down to chew the fat. Idleness is a virtue too few of us willingly indulge. The Yankee spirit of mercantilism, imbued with an overdose of Puritanism—always alive and well, even in places like supposedly sybaritic Los Angeles—keeps us moving. But on a sunny morning in a small front garden roughly twenty feet deep, James is at rest. He doesn't live at MLK1101, but he's there, taking the pulse of anyone who walks by along a forbidding stretch of Martin Luther King Jr. Boulevard. Less than half a mile away is the original Agricultural Park, hub of gambling and public debauchery before the city's prigs sanitized it, shutting down the horse racing track and rechristening it Exposition Park while timing the opening of its sunken rose garden to coincide with William Mulholland's turning the spigot on for the delivery of Owens Valley water in 1913. James greets everyone cruising by, speaking over the constant road noise, which, on a boulevard that was wide enough to accommodate the space shuttle *Endeavour* on its twelve-mile trek from LAX to the park's California Science Center, comes in overpowering spurts of tire treads rumbling on blacktop. James, as if inspired by the traffic rather than put off by it, has countless tales about vehicles: road trips and motor failures on his classic 1990s Ducati (now in storage, set aside for his daughter, who, he admits, probably won't ever ride the motorcycle), the Japan-built Bianchi bicycle he's currently riding and rebuilding ("29-inch rear tire, 26-inch front, Shimano cassettes, double-butted frame"), and the E-type Jaguars his father, a dentist, once owned. He dispenses words with a New York twang, touting his career as a graphic designer and photographer, musing about the kinds of businesses that might succeed in the ground-floor retail space behind him.

All units are accessed via exterior walkways that function as balconies and outdoor space.

A sense of liberty pervades the boulevard: Perhaps this busy atmosphere actually promotes unofficial and unsanctioned expression, and only needed the small public plaza James occupies to summon it forth. The streets adjacent to Martin Luther King Jr. Boulevard—officially changed from Santa Barbara Avenue on January 15, 1983, to commemorate King's birthday—contain the memory of the untamed and freewheeling. At the core of African American Los Angeles, which was marginalized economically and politically for decades, this area always was a bit ill-disposed to the bespoke, uptown, tidy version of the city governed a few miles north, in downtown. This anti-snobbery crops up as high culture, and low. Philip Guston, Harold Lehman, and Jackson Pollock were a troika of art students who attended Manual Arts High School, a block away, and got tossed out for their unruly political misdeeds (all three would eventually develop their artist language while working with the most revolutionary of the revolutionary Mexican muralists, David Alfaro Siqueiros). Equally rebellious, in a mock-comic (and likely wholly unintentional) way, is the "So LA" smoke shop, a few doors west and across the six-lane concourse. The double entendre nags for a resolution: Is there an implied comma between "So" and "LA"? Would that render the shop's name a kind of two-word concession speech to the city that had absorbed one more exhausted pilgrim into its insatiable maw? Or, sans comma, maybe it boldly proclaims its allegiance to a street that, but for its name, is too easily dismissed as ugly, uncared for, down-on-its-heels poor, and sorely unkempt. Maybe without that comma "So LA" refers to the unabashed embrace of a neighborhood that, yes, has razor wire stretched along its alleys and suffers the incessant, sibilant hiss of compressed air coming from its no-name tire repair shops, but also has block after block of intact, pre–World War I clapboard bungalows and row after row of Empire palms providing deft vertical counterpoint to the otherwise endless horizontal plane.

The L-shaped building wraps along two sides of the lot, allowing every apartment to receive ample natural light and efficient cross-ventilation, while ample interior courtyard space accessible from the street helps it function as a public square.

It's a curious building, man. I love it.
—James (neighborhood resident)

MLK and Vermont Avenue intersect at one of the true visual launch-points for the city, a place from which you can see the rising slope of Los Angeles as it makes its way to its greatest backdrop, the San Gabriel Mountains. Here, the cross section of blue sky, which is impossibly visible, has a way of turning even harsh reality into a kind of ephemeral luminosity. Every building, including MLK1101, is much too low to the ground—and those palm trees too wispy—to blot out the sunlight that has always been the city's greatest muse.

Like so much else in south Los Angeles, grace is poised on the tip of the grit, in uneasy balance that simply does not yield to passing judgment. No one on these streets is going to bother to pause to convert anyone else to their self-avowed orthodoxy or, if it comes to that, to their dress code or late-model car code. Or, in the doing, be taken especially seriously. Maybe that's why this small public plaza becomes a place of tolerance and welcome. An oasis where someone like James—clearly a man without a particular portfolio or the best of luck, lately—can kibbitz with passersby who, like him, feel no desire to take possession, proclaim ownership, or avow anything more than a simple "hello."

Strong geometry helps drive pedestrians to the entry point for the outdoor living room, elevated from street level.

BRUSH PARK

→ P. 257

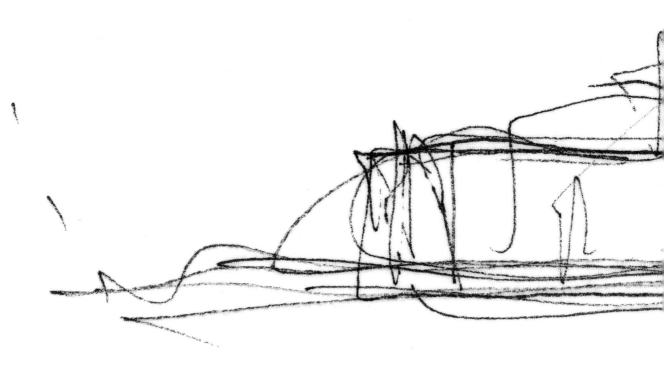

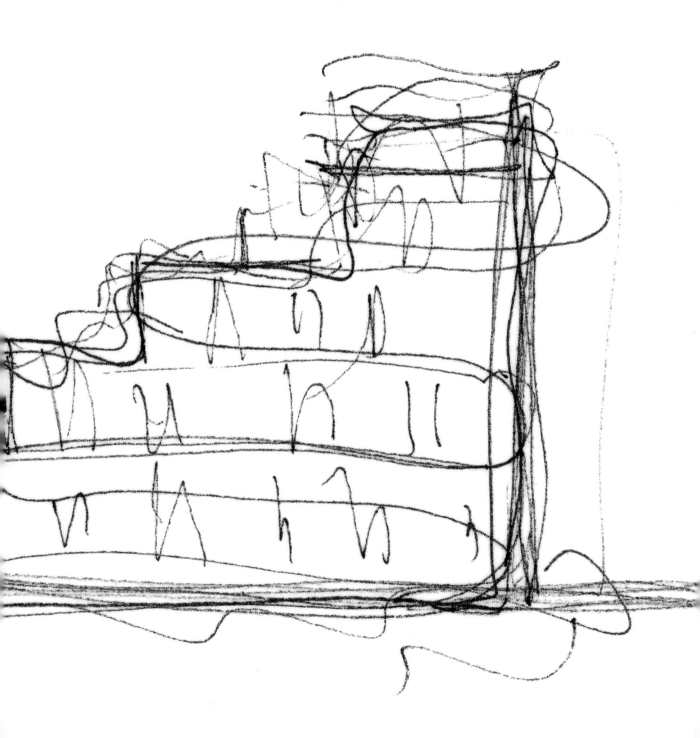

A walk through Brush Park: Empty lots, abandoned houses. Tumbling walls, stacks of bricks piled and forgotten. Slate mansards, dentil eaves, copper dormers, gaping roofs, dangling beams. Quarried stepping stones, rising to nowhere. Arched lintels, towering chimneys. Blackened oriented strand board, delaminating. Impassible rusted steel plates guarding blinkered rooms. Cast iron lampposts two stories high, the solitary adornments of empty parkways. Purple palettes of wildflowers, raccoon-tough saplings. This eerie patch between Woodward Avenue on the west, Beaubien Boulevard on the east, Mack Avenue on the north, and the Fisher Freeway on the south, was formerly the "Little Paris of the Midwest." Beginning in the 1850s, roughly 300 homes were built in Brush Park, brick-and-wood mansions of the city's elites, who were drawn to the twenty-five unevenly spaced rectangular blocks just one mile from the very epicenter of Detroit at Fort and Griswold Streets.

Like the city, Brush Park begins with France. Detroit was founded in the first year of the eighteenth century by the French explorer and trader Antoine de la Mothe Cadillac (a name that truly had a second act). He named this outpost after the river it faces: known to cartographers of the time as "le détroit du Lac Érié," or "the strait of Lake Erie," the waterway connecting Lake Erie to Lake Huron via Lake St. Clair. Cadillac gave the Marquis de Beauharnois, a French naval officer who served as governor of New France—aka Canada—a slice of the new township. It was a ribbon farm beginning at water's edge and stretching almost six miles inland.

Brick, a historic material used for many of the area's original Victorian homes, reappears again on Edmund 200, one of LOHA's four buildings that anchor the 8.4-acre Brush Park revitalization site.

Red metal, harking back to Detroit's industrial past, injects color into the neighborhood while a unique folded form pulls the massing of Studio 320 back from the street.

Onto that and adjacent farms were etched names that became the streets of Detroit: Arnault, Beauregard, Bourbon, Cadieux, Cadillac, Campau, Charlevoix, Chavet, Dequindre, Frontenac, Fournier, Gratiot, Guyon, Hubbard, Labrosse, Lafayette, Lamothe, LaSalle, Livernois, Marquette, Montagne, Navarre, Piquette, Pontchartrain, Radisson, Renaud, Richard, Riopelle, and Rivard. And, of course, the eastern boundary of Brush Park, Beaubien Street, which is a portmanteau of *beau bien*, "beautiful property," a shorthand for the location of an estate.

When Elijah Brush, a Vermont lawyer who became Detroit's second mayor, handed his son Edmund the land the marquis had received more than a century before, the ambitious subdivider scratched new avenues and streets into Augustus Woodward's 1807 hexagonal grid (inspired by L'Enfant's baroque radial layout for Washington, DC). Most he named after family or prominent locals: Adelaide, Alfred, Benton, Canfield, Edmund, Eliot, Willis, Winder.

Building John R 2660 steps down from five stories to two to align with the scale of the Victorian architecture across the street.

These Yankee names, like the French names, were destined to become relics. Most of Brush's opulent borough was gone less than fifty years after the last mansion was built in 1906. This thanks to Albert Kahn, the great architect of the first-ever clear-span factories that made Detroit into an industrial metropolis. By the time of the Great Depression, Brush Park had become a Black community, its working families employed in the automobile industry. Then what's known as the Race Riot of 1943 broke out; in the ensuing decade the City of Detroit had a concerted policy of "slum clearance." Much of Brush Park was bulldozed. It became an island of abandonment, a few decaying houses and apartments marooned among cleared lots.

What was left, until the recent effort to revive Brush Park, was a skein of vacant streets and deserted sidewalks with treeless parkways sandwiched between. It's those parkways, perhaps, that echo most eloquently with the ghosts of Brush Park. The barren soil masks an unwritten convergence. There, the terrible fate

Cedar panels clad this building in a nod to Detroit's historic wooden architecture, while modern floor-to-ceiling windows control privacy for residents.

Strategic cuts in Brush 2665 mediate scale to respond to context while allowing for residential density in a way that still allows the neighborhood to feel open.

of Detroit's 400,000 towering American elms that once formed cathedrals of shade over the city's streets—over Brush Park's streets—overlaps with the bloodiest urban rebellion in United States history, the 1967 Detroit Riot. That battle during the "long, hot summer of 1967" pitted the city's notoriously brutal and bigoted police against an African American community that could no longer contain decades of pent-up anger over systematic racism and enforced poverty. By that same year, most of the hundreds of elm saplings planted in the 1880s in Brush Park had become blighted victims of Dutch elm disease. Not long after the riot had left its deep, bitter wound, the city suddenly showed up and clear-cut the stately, 120-foot-tall trees, further decimating an already devastated Brush Park. To some, both actions appeared to have the same motive: the city removing the least of its residents. A scar was etched into living memory.

Four and a half decades on, that scar is a fragmentary trace, noticeable along the narrow, barren parkways of Brush Park. The contemporary nothing that is there is a strikingly blatant clue as to how lush and vital the neighborhood had once been too. Still, at little more than three feet wide—they were originally closer to five feet when the elms were first planted and spaced forty feet apart—some sidewalks are now dotted with young plane trees. Which seems strangely fitting: Napoleon, who ordered the lining of France's roads with plane trees to shade his marching troops, was the name of the Brush Park street wiped away to build a freeway as part of the slum clearance that slowly ignited the city's 1967 riot. There is talk in Detroit of removing those freeways. Maybe, too, through those juvenile plane trees, those skinny parkways, those empty lots, the past city grid will serve as a positive map for the future.

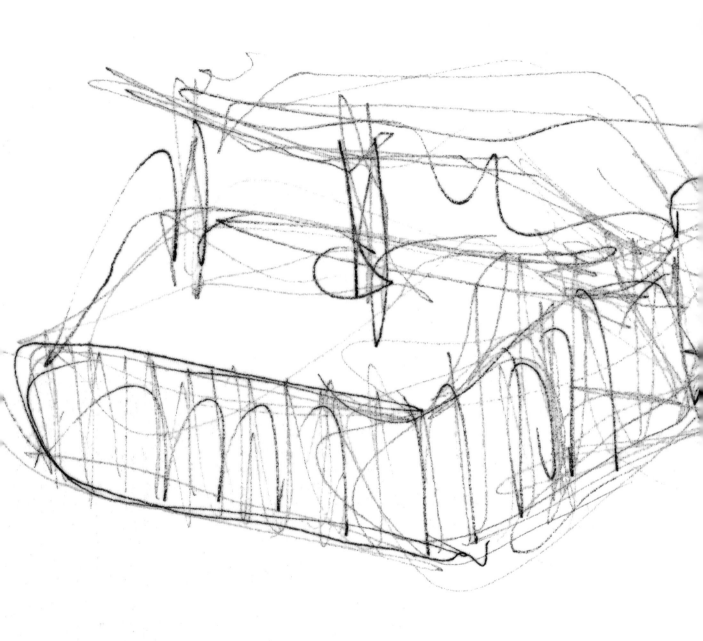

→ P. 258

UCSB SAN JOAQUIN STUDENT HOUSING

Whole swaths of California are unsettled, places seemingly unoccupied, with no one for miles around. Others are built up, larded over, yet still unsettled. The landscape—the geology, biology, archaeological record as the faded footprint of human habitation—asserts itself unexpectedly in uncanny proportion to the conditions on the ground. Nowhere is this more true than on the Santa Barbara campus of the University of California. Unlike older universities, many of the UC campuses were conceived on fresh paper, as two-dimensional site plans rather than clusters of buildings gradually coalescing within the city of origin. UCSB was also a preconceived idea superimposed on a presumed tabula rasa. But on this gorgeous headland between Goleta and Isla Vista— the first a bedroom community with million-dollar-plus homes, the second a student ghetto with unaffordable rents—the school has been grafted onto a geography that over two hundred and fifty years, from conquest to complacency, seems to be a site prepped for willful amnesia.

This mesa where the school emerged, not quite whole cloth, is a rare spot on the extraordinary, and extraordinarily beautiful, 840-mile-long California coastline. It was long home to the Chumash, whose settlements extended from Malibu to San Luis Obispo to the Channel Islands, off Santa Barbara's coast, and inland to the San Joaquin Valley, and land eventually appropriated for UCSB happened to be on the mostly densely populated Chumash settlement in the region, perhaps the largest native settlement in the state. The area was first explored by the Spanish expedition led by Juan Rodríguez Cabrillo; in 1542, he encountered about 1,000 American Indian people here. More than 200 years

Open courtyards, ample windows, outdoor access, and green space encourage social interaction among students.

later, in August of 1769, Gaspar de Portolá's expedition in Alta California encountered a large bay among thick stands of oak about fourteen miles north of present-day Santa Barbara, lined with Chumash villages. The bay—an estuary protected by a crescent-shaped sandbar—surrounded an island, named Mescaltitlan by the Spaniards, that was occupied by the largest of the villages. Portolá's diarist, Fray Juan Crespi, wrote, "Seems as though all the lushness in the world lies there …" adding, "This is all a Good Land." An all-too-familiar fate met the Chumash, whose name means "shell bead money maker" or "seashell people." Enslaved into mission life, they succumbed to forced labor and smallpox, and when California was made a state in 1850, it became legal to kill American Indians. Before Portolá arrived there had been about 22,000 Chumash; by 1910, there were fewer than forty.

The bay, which in reality was a slough, a shallow wetland, lasted only a few decades longer. First came torrential rains in 1861 that sent silt and uprooted trees and mountain chaparral seaward, sealing off the freshwater wetland from the Pacific. The vast lagoon turned overnight into a shallow, muddy marsh. The surrounding lands were farmed in the succeeding decades. Then, in 1928, adventurous aviators laid an airstrip on a cow pasture, which by 1941 became

Passive design strategies and innovative, off-the-shelf durable material choices result in a project that is more efficient and economical than standard new construction.

the Santa Barbara Municipal Airport. That was built by slicing the top off Mescaltitlan Island, the archaeologically rich earth used as fill to convert marshlands to runways. Less than a year later, the United States entered World War II and requisitioned Goleta's airport for a Marine airbase. Mescaltitlan was reduced to a mound to build more runways.

And there the mosquito-ridden slough stagnated: a marsh at low tide, criss-crossed by rivulets and muddy lanes, a trio of wide-fingered waterways at high tide, and a year-round sanctuary for one hundred bird species and an equal number of plant species. The slough became an impediment to development, however, so it was slated to be sliced in two by a new freeway for the convenience of the university, with much of its remaining acreage earmarked for a mobile home park, an artificial lake, a harbor, and a marina. None of this happened: the storm of late 1960s environmentalism blew it away.

The landscape that once supported a civilization clings to a precarious existence, and is visible out of the corner of your eye. Across El Colegio Road,
three-tenths of a mile south of the Isla Vista student housing complex, lies Del
Sol Vernal Pool Reserve. A pockmark that fills seasonally with water in winter
and early spring, it's an itsy-bitsy piece of Indigenous habitat, tawny brown,
usually dried up, almost forgettable in its utter lack of scenic beauty. When wet,
spike rushes push up through the still water, and Pacific tree frogs, loud
croaking creatures, breed and lay eggs. Farther on, the shores of the Goleta
Slough Marine Conservation Area—all that's left of the bay the Chumash
once occupied—are lined in oak woodlands, sage scrub, and grasslands. You
see great blue herons nesting in their noisome rookeries, hear black-crowned
night herons' barking squawks, catch views of Canada geese migrating along
the Pacific Flyway, and if truly lucky, you glimpse the yellow highlights of the
endangered Belding's savannah sparrow.

Paths for bikes, a popular transportation option on the UCSB campus, circle the dorms.

The slough is, in fact, one of a few surviving salt marshes on the West Coast, approximately 75 percent of them having been paved over into residential or commercial areas. Decimated for places, like those immediately north of the dorm, seen through a scrim of pines: four-bedroom, four-bathroom houses, built in YR2000, on streets blandly called Willowgrove, Sweet Rain, Poppyfield, Sweetwater, Woodleaf, Buttonwood, Silkberry, and Coolbrook. Made-up names, indicating nothing orienting about this slightly elevated plat that once lipped the former bay. Does Silkberry refer to the imported floss silk trees, *Ceiba speciosa*, native to the tropical and subtropical forests of South America? Does Buttonwood refer to *Conocarpus erectus*, a species of misplaced mangrove shrub? The Chumash called slough *Sitiptip*, "Place of much salt." No doubt if we translated other Chumash words for the area, *Qwa', 'Alkash, misɨk, Heliyɨk, palt, quwa', 'anisqu 'oyo, tiptip, 'alwat'alam, S'axpilil*, they'd prove equally more apt.

In the 1950s, the university took the high, dry plateau on the bluffs above Goleta Point, drafting the Los Angeles corporate modernists Pereira & Luckman to lay out a campus from scratch. They introduced patterned, sand-blasted concrete textile block brickwork on the first buildings, adding volcanic ash aggregate to color the cement cinnamon—though it looks more pink than light brown. So, students must navigate two worlds, worlds apart. Superimposed structure, wildlife sanctuary. There may be no uniting them, but there can be rapprochement. All one needs to do is tumble out of bed and wander a few blocks, and there you are, in the presence of the past, in the presence of the natural order, in the presence of the irrepressibly unsettled.

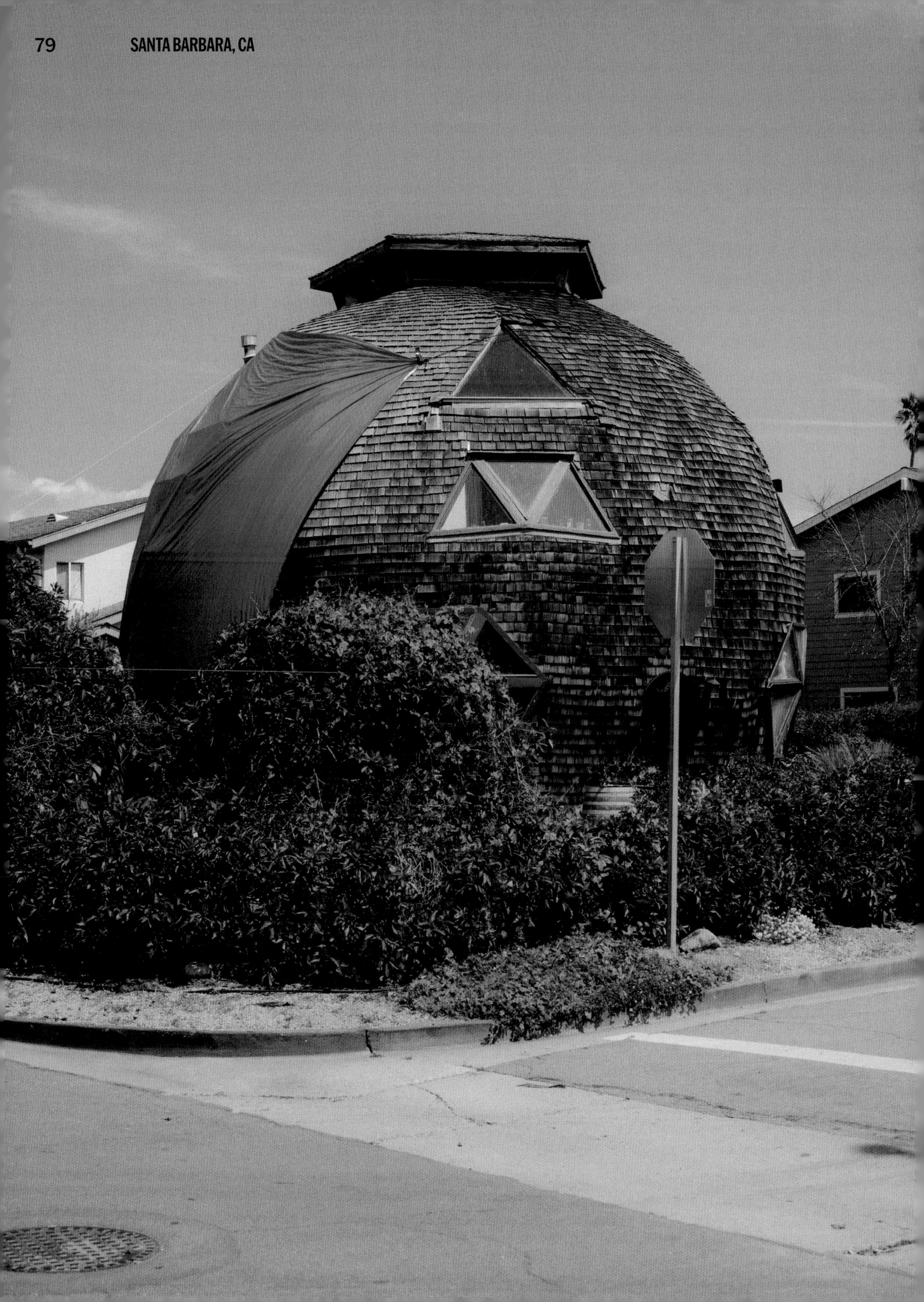

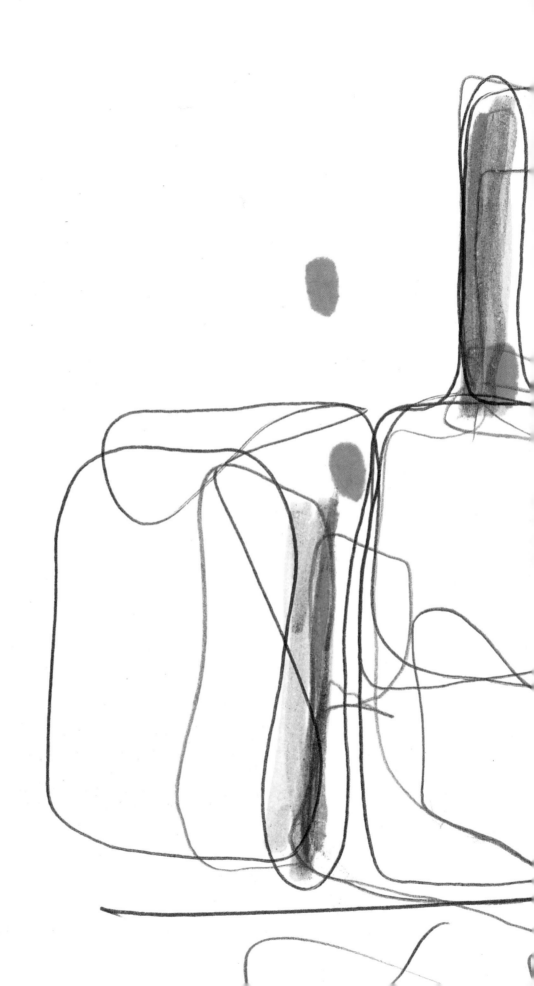

→ P. 259

WILLOUGHBY 7917

A rectangular exterior form that maximizes an infill lot's area contains eight residential spaces differentiated in part by cutouts, balconies, and windows of various sizes.

The inspiration for good architecture is not great architecture. It is just architecture. Sometimes even bad architecture, more often ordinary, no-name, absentee architecture. The imagination, it seems, can land on the unexpected, new, even the beautiful, through the spurs of the mundane. It's not exactly an accident, but more like a corollary of the truth that the prosaic is the unacknowledged architect of the city.

Look no further than a marooned corner of West Hollywood at the intersection of Willoughby and Hayworth Avenues. Here is a continuous turf of discontinuity. Straight through the 1950s, when the area was invisibly partitioned between the City of Los Angeles and the County of Los Angeles, the sixteen square blocks of narrow north-south streets and even skinnier east-west roads emanating from the intersection were all duplexes and fourplexes of the 1910s and 1920s, with a smattering of eightplexes, neatly spaced eleven in a row on each side of a block.

All that metamorphosized into a conglomerate starting in the early 1960s and continues to perform new feats of morphological accretion through the present day. Here's what you encounter: a two-story, dingbat, lot-line-to-lot line, ticky-tacky with a soft story subterranean garage next to a surviving

Stainless-steel mesh suspended four inches away from the building's exterior surface creates a moiré effect and is meant to support vining vegetation.

Multi-floor units that shift over and above neighboring units, as opposed to stacking directly one on top of another, create dynamic and adaptable spaces for living.

one-story Spanish colonial revival (whose chief observable remaining "revival" characteristic is a parapet capped with clay tiles), next to an asphalt-shingle mansard accidentally-on-purpose adhered to the top of a stucco box (Hollywood Regency sans Hollywood, sans Regency), sandwiched between twin Cape Cod clapboard condos adorned with gambrel roofs. Around the corner stands a postmodern four-story with a standing seam sheet metal shed roof and perforated metal awnings impersonating Parisian Art Nouveau glass canopies. At another corner, a Baron Haussmann Second Empire concoction, excruciatingly detailed down to the oeil-de-boeuf dormer windows, slate roofs, and grilles. Down the block, an Art Deco with a miniaturized movie marquee. Up the block, a pair of second-floor stucco verandas with exaggerated scalloped overhangs complement a concave green mosaic panel, in a decorative scheme worthy of *The Jetsons*. So it goes. There's even a Tuscan-church-façade apartment, with a trio of calla lily balconies hung between three arches supporting a low, featureless pediment.

Then there are the trees, changing species house by house, apartment by apartment. Magnolia, camphor, palm, juniper, floss silk, flowering pear, jacaranda, mimosa, sycamore, tabebuia (pink trumpet tree). Some appeared to have been pollarded, others merely hacked. Some are dead. Some evergreen, some deciduous. In bloom, they're a spectacle of pinks and purples and yellows. The hedges and fences, too, are polyglot and polymorphic. Boxwood, ficus, and privet (one at least twelve feet high, completely concealing the shanty it towers above). White picket fences, low stucco walls, redbrick and off-the-shelf black iron fences, motorized sliding wooden gates (protecting a front yard paved entirely for parking), a schoolyard hemmed in a chain-link fence with green plastic slats woven on the diagonal through the galvanized metal mesh.

Somehow, it all fits together, like a white-on-white jigsaw puzzle—in the end, it doesn't really matter what goes where, what detail any individual piece contains. In a place like this, liberated even from the confines of a prevailing vernacular, you're free. Given the demands of a client who needs a box—to maximize the number of square feet that can be built on a lot—you're inspired to make that box into something more than a prism pasted with gewgaws, inject a visual pause into the melee. So, this three-story gray box, at first glance, looks like a three-story gray box. In fact, it is a downright simple set of flat surfaces, carved away in certain spots, interspersed with oversize windows. Its modesty is posed. On closer inspection, the grayish skin reveals itself as a stainless-steel mesh, held four inches away from the exterior walls by stainless-steel dowels, each panel tied to the adjacent with twists of stainless-steel wire. When the Western sun is snared in its rippled surface, a trompe l'oeil emerges. Voilà: You've got a building wrapped in a cloak of moiré. The building shimmers, silky, satiny, soft.

That's it. Out of the ordinary the extraordinary.

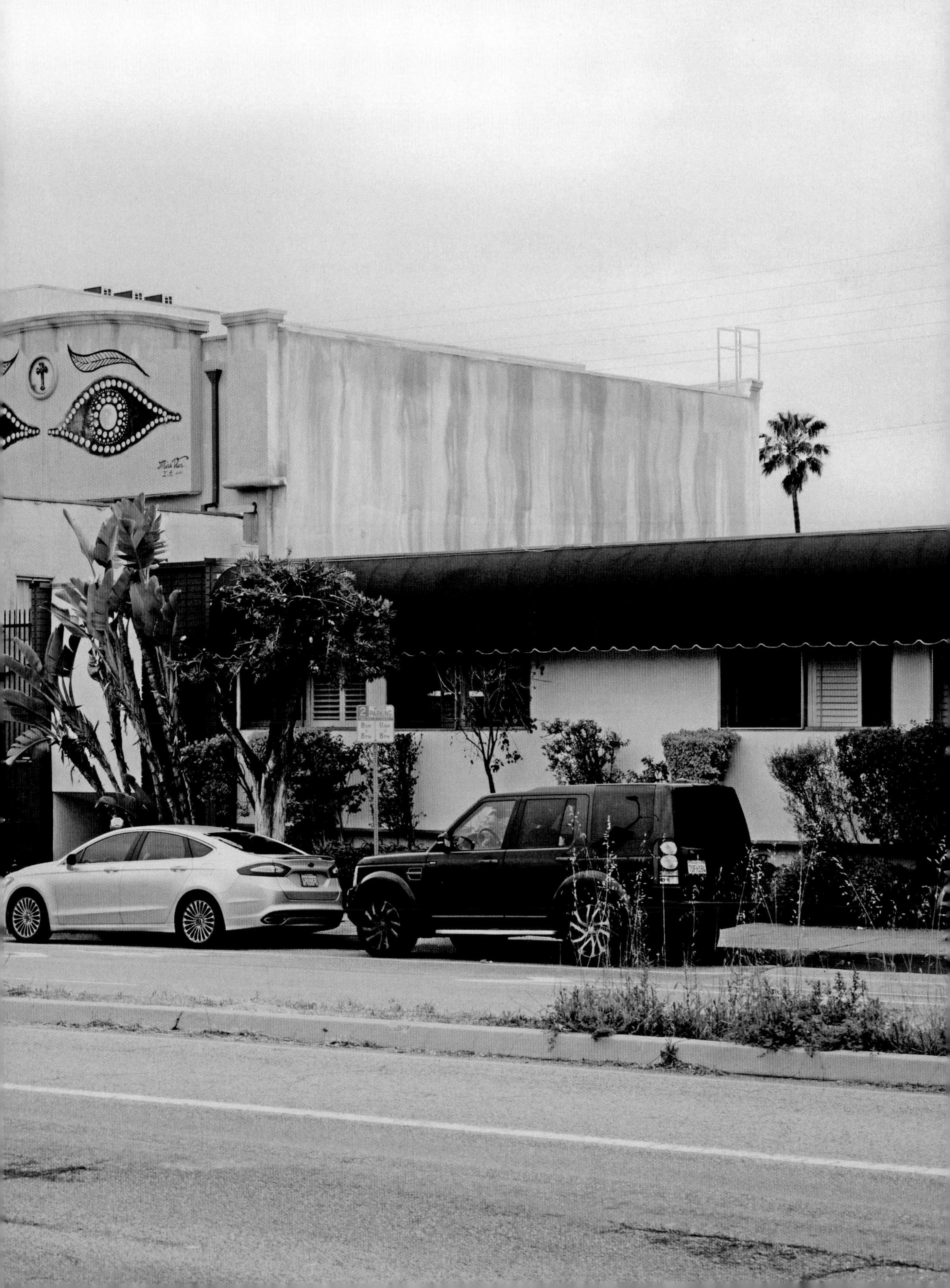
2 PARKING

CLOVERDALE 749

→ P. 260

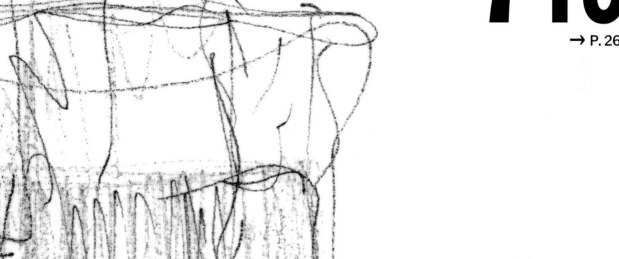

On February 28, 1922, a block-long mantle of eight-inch-thick concrete, laid down with parallel sidewalks and graced with cast concrete street lighting standards, was given the name Cloverdale—bucolic for a street in an otherwise barren barley field whose lots were subdivided but undeveloped, lending the place an eerie air, as if abandoned before anyone had even managed to build a home on one of the vacant lots. The name Cloverdale lacked a specific reference, appended to these 570 feet from Wilshire Boulevard to Eighth Street, so it seems, because another stretch of road farther south corresponding to the same longitude already was called Cloverdale. Perhaps clover sprouted on the empty land that gently sloped southwest toward the wind gap at Ballona Creek, which accounted for the summer breezes that spread inland from the ocean. Perhaps not.

But Cloverdale was sufficiently evocative to convey a hint of Anglo-Saxon ancestry, derived as it was from the far east of the Yorkshire Dales, in northern England. The street name was, in fact, part of a sales pitch for a place that didn't exist—not yet. A total of sixteen streets would be cut to intersect with a dirt road that a prescient and canny realtor and land speculator A. W. Ross shelled out $54,000 to buy in 1920, along with eighteen acres on the south side of what would become the westward extension of the city's most important street, Wilshire Boulevard.

The building's light-colored façade fits with the neighborhood's predominantly stucco structures while indicating a move toward the contemporary and reducing solar heat load.

The focus is on the layered elements, and the commitment to exterior access was key to this project. These elements generally go out the window as they can be considered superfluous but to us they are critical for a robust and ecologically driven project.

This one-mile stretch became the "Miracle Mile": Ross had seen the future, and it was the automobile. His genius was to build the nation's first linear commercial strip, dedicated to commuters willing to drive five miles to a boulevard lined with elegant Art Deco buildings, high-end department stores, food marts, restaurants, and movie theaters.

Yet the label Miracle Mile, like Cloverdale, was another instance of prestidigitation by nomenclature. You could conjure an entirely new precinct simply by manipulating names. Before Ross arrived on the scene, the area was part of Allan Hancock's chunk of the old Spanish Rancho La Brea, where Hancock had discovered rich deposits of oil. Hundreds and hundreds of acres became pincushions punctured with oil derricks, making Hancock a very rich man. It would have been natural to assume that the nickname derived from the thousands of barrels of oil—and millions of dollars—pumped out of the tar soils where the neighborhood sprang up and where, to this day,

Pushing circulation to the exterior reduces the need for climate-controlled, artificially lit internal hallways and increases a sense of urban dynamism.

some lucky landowners still collect oil royalties. But that would have been too direct: Ross originally called his development the much duller "Wilshire Boulevard Center." Supposedly, Ross was describing his vision when a friend commented, "From the way you talk, A.W., one would think this is really a miracle mile." A promoter's dream, the name stuck.

So it went: Wilshire, which would become the spine of big-business Los Angeles, flanked by the homes of its wealthiest citizens, who kept moving west, was named for the "millionaire-socialist" real estate magnate Gaylord Wilshire. He befriended fellow anti-capitalists Jack London, George Bernard Shaw, and Upton Sinclair. The La Brea Tar Pits itself is a circumlocution. The redundant name in which *la brea*—Spanish for "the tar"—means our standard moniker for them, the La Brea Tar Pits, translates to "The Tar Tar Pits" or "The Tar Pits Tar Pits." Gaspar de Portolá, when he rode by on the Spanish expedition in 1769, called the asphalt geysers in the swampy Miracle Mile, "Los Volcanes de Brea" (The Tar Volcanoes), which at least was descriptive of an actual phenomenon. Then there was Cahuenga Boulevard, now called Cochran (an appropriately Scottish surname), yet another linguistic mix-up; a Spanish-sounding invented word to evoke the romance of the bygone ranchos but actually a bastardization of the Tongva *Kawee'nga*, the name for the settlement near what is today Universal City. Some translate it as "place of the hill" but UCLA linguistics professor Pamela Munro says it's "place of the fox." The Miracle Mile doesn't have much of a hill, and maybe there were once foxes, but the Tongva used the asphalt from the pits as a glue to waterproof baskets and caulk their plank canoes. Just two streets in the area have any verisimilitude: La Brea, two blocks east of Cloverdale, started out as a service road for oil prospectors, and Masselin Avenue was named for a French sailor who bought 120 acres and ran sheep on open land through which the eponymous street now runs.

The Miracle Mile has always been a boulevard of mishmashed dreams. A scant year after Cloverdale was named, the Archway Plan was announced. Designed by Aurele Vermeulen, who'd laid out Bel Air, it was intended to make Wilshire Boulevard into a 230-foot-wide street—"the world's finest thoroughfare"—crossed by eleven archways and dotted with seven obelisks, an equal number of fountains, and one enormous Capitol-dome-shaped hall. National and international competitions were to be held to choose the "best artists and sculptors" to outfit the arches, obelisks, and fountains. Cloverdale would have landed somewhere between the National Poets Monument, the Natural History Fountain (at Hancock Park), the Pioneer Arch, and an obelisk consecrated "to builders."

If this is the backdrop, where names and places are largely confections, is it possible to implant an anticonfection? Can a corrugated white metal cuboid hexahedron, carved away strategically to reveal black stucco walls and a prominent spiral staircase, adorned with nothing more than a plain gray concrete block planter and aluminum block lettering spelling out "7-4-9-C-L-O-V-E-R-D-A-L-E" become permanent? Be more than ephemeral? Can metal rising straight up from the ground be a simulacrum, an extrusion giving life and expression to that very ground? Can a building with zero pretenses become the origin of place? Why not.

White metal sheathing acts as a veil that at once conceals and reveals private and public spheres—
and the interaction between them—in a volume that maximizes the possibilities for restrictive urban zoning.

SL11024

→ P. 261

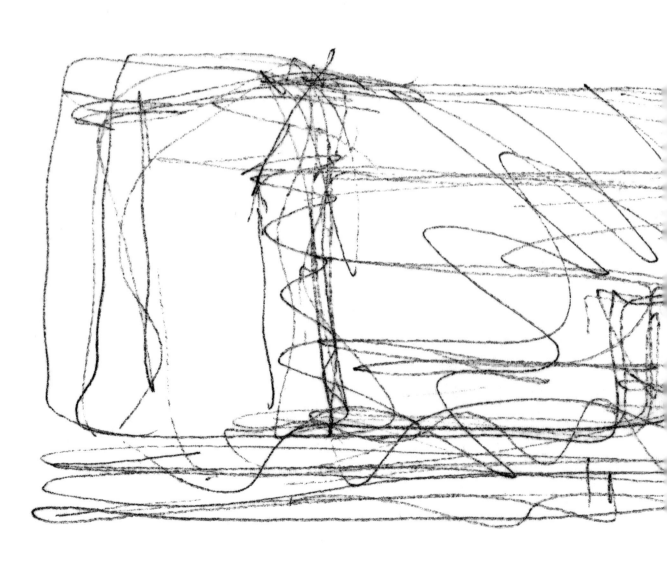

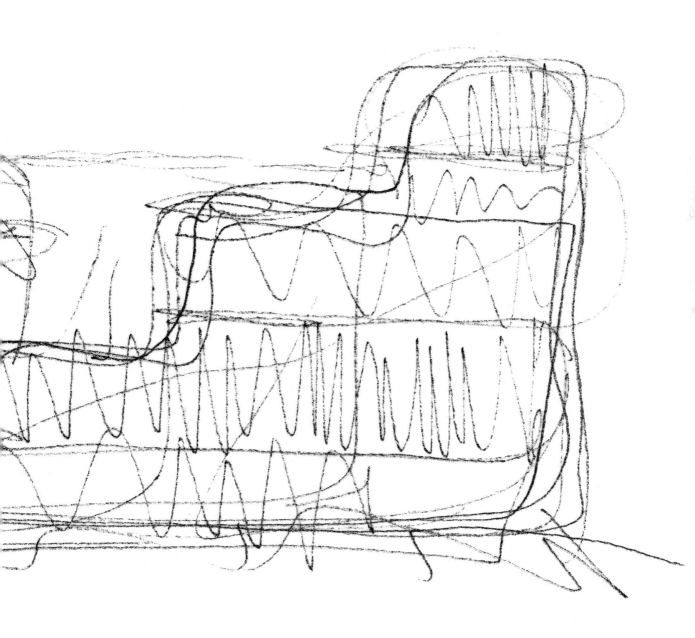

Universities have traditionally sprung up where groups of students have congregated around great scholars—as with Oxford, a bustling early medieval settlement catapulted into fame as the first home of secular learning in the English-speaking world. Earlier, ancient Greeks brought formal learning to their Sicilian colony at Syracuse. But as with so much else in Los Angeles, the historical process was reversed: first came the university, then came the town. Or, in this case, the village: Westwood.

Not that a town hadn't been planned for the rolling hills on the 3,000-acre ranch originally called Rancho San José de Buenos Aires—"ranch of the beautiful breezes." In the 1880s, the town of Sunset was platted, but it went bankrupt in 1891 and the ownership reverted to John Wolfskill, who renamed the spread Wolfskill Ranch. In 1919 he sold to a successful department store magnate, Arthur Letts, who conceived a new subdivision intended to become a money-making, auto-centric village surrounded by well-to-do single-family homes and low-lying apartments. But Letts's holding remained open lands where cattle and horses had been grazed since the early 1800s and where mule-drawn plows still cut furrows for local farmers in the early 1910s and 1920s.

The Westwood origin story really begins with a tidy deal engineered to enrich a private developer by making it appear as if he was doing a charitable deed. Arthur Letts, like every other real estate speculator in Southern California, knew that the University of California was looking to build a new campus for its "Southern Branch" (then called Los Angeles State Normal School, located not far from downtown, on Vermont Avenue). University regent Edward Dickson, who also happened to own and edit the *Los Angeles Express* newspaper,

The student housing building accommodates a wedge-shaped lot and a 50-foot grade change.

Cement board painted in shades of vivid green grounds the massing along the slope and indicates circulation areas and gathering spaces such as roof terraces and courtyards.

agreed with Letts that if the university landed on the ranch, the land around it could be built up into "an ideal college town—complete with a business section, student housing, and restricted residential area." Letts died, but his son-in-law's real estate firm, the Janss Investment Company, which now owned the acreage, sold 375 acres to the adjacent cities of Los Angeles, Santa Monica, and Beverly Hills at the bargain price of $1.2 million—about a quarter of its value—but still nearly covering the entire original investment of $1.5 million. The cities, whose voters in 1925 had passed bond issues to pay for the site, promptly donated it to the state. The payoff was almost instantaneous. Within four days of the announcement that UCLA was coming, though the area contained nothing more than an observation tower with an illuminated sign spelling out "Westwood," Janss had sold roughly 275 lots, raking in $1 million.

The design of the new campus was handed to architect brothers Allison & Allison, who set out to transform the empty rolling hills and deep ravines into a romantic vision of Romanesque Revival. UCLA emerged around a quartet of buildings with clay-tile roofs and red and white brick course-work walls, as if plucked from the picturesque hilltops of Lombardy. Westwood, under Janss's direction, would explode with the university's boomtown appearance; it peddled a similar fantasy via a camera-ready Mediterranean village, outfitted with domes and paseos, patios, and courtyards. Towers, which were intended to catch the eyes of motorists traveling by in the "fast moving traffic" of Wilshire Boulevard, dominated the skyline. Four Spanish Revival gas stations, each with its own tower, lined up in a neat row: Richfield with its soaring eagle, Mobil with its winged red Pegasus, Chevron with its geometric bars, 76 with its illuminated numbers. Sears, Roebuck & Co. had its tower, too, as did the Fox Village Theater, a seventeen-story "wedding cake" tower capped by a three-sided spire sporting a blue-and-gold neon sign (UCLA's mascot colors). Janss crowned the fictional narrative with an office building outfitted with a massive dome finished in polished Moorish-style aqua and white zigzag-patterned mosaic tiles and gold leaf.

The clean, white metal panels of the façade respond to Richard Neutra's famed modernist apartment building directly across the street.

This one was unique in terms of its revered location. To design a project that has artistry and respects its historical neighbor is both challenging and rewarding.

The Janss Investment Company's map of the new university township marks Hilgard Avenue, on the eastern boundary of the campus, as "Sorority Row," while hills west of campus, near the athletic fields, were decreed "Fraternity Row." There, in 1936, at the precipitous, pointy convergence of Strathmore Drive and Levering Avenue, the city's trailblazing Black architect, Paul Williams, built Kappa Sigma fraternity house. In keeping with the Mediterranean motif of Westwood, he produced an elongated stucco mansion with a gabled, tile roof, deep-set windows, and, as befitted the eclectic notes of Los Angeles architecture, with more-or-less jalousie shutters that are mock Georgian but rather suited to a mock Tuscan.

Williams's fraternity house had sat empty for two years when, in 1997, a non-profit Catholic educational organization called Tilden Study Center bought the property, hoping to remodel it. Fate determined otherwise: the building had deteriorated and been so infested with termites that, in the words of Tilden's cofounder, Carlos Alejano, it had become "just one of those romantic things, but in reality ... useless."

An unintended irony was lurking in Alejano's comment. Westwood had, indeed, been intended as a sort of three-dimensional roman à clef—a nostalgic novel populated by real people and real places but borrowed from the towns and styles of the Mediterranean. But on the hillsides west of UCLA, something else emerged. From the drafting tables of European immigrants, modernism took form. And, lo and behold, modernism came to govern the future of the spot where Williams had conceived his narrative-conforming Spanish Colonial Revival. For, directly across the street, a year after Kappa Sigma opened, Richard Neutra did something entirely new. He built a pathbreaking eight-unit courtyard garden apartment complex, a cubist sculpture with white stucco walls, sliding ribbon windows with silver trim, and totally flat roofs. At first, no one would rent the apartments; they were regarded as "cold," "austere," "industrial," "hospital architecture." Enter designers Charles and Ray Eames, who arrived in Los Angeles in 1941, moved right in, and decreed the setting perfect: "a beautifully clean and simple shell [that] imposes no style on the tenants, but leaves them free to create their own surroundings through color, texture, use of area and equipment needed for everyday life and activities."

Neutra's mantras that landscape and greenery were not luxuries but necessities and that the size of a home did not determine the quality of life lived within, triumphed over all the pseudo-style architecture grafted onto the mythical place of Westwood. So, when 11024 Strathmore was reborn—Williams's frat house was razed in 2010—the apartment building embraced the core of the modernist émigré's philosophy. Almost nowhere else in the recent history of Westwood would this be in evidence: outdoor spaces, public arenas, indoor apartments with through-and-through spaces, stepped volumes tracing the natural contours of the street, and a color scheme of pale greens and vivid white, signaling that even the most cash-strapped, indentured students deserve the highest quality of design.

Layered massing helps the building feel as if it cascades naturally down the hillside while windows and voids in various sizes add shadow and movement.

SANDI SIMON CENTER FOR DANCE AT CHAPMAN UNIVERSITY

→ P. 262

127

In the town of Orange, it was always about sunlight: "When we dig down deep into the mellow earth and find plant life in rare abundance, and feel the sun's gentle warmth as it filters its life-giving rays through a producing season of almost 365 days in a year, and when we see all nature aglow with the hope of Spring lasting through the four seasons, and blending into each other as gently as the fading of a crimson sunset at the close of a Summer's day, then we know we have found the chosen land where fear of want will not disturb our dreams, nor failure of crops still our expectations." So said D.W. McDannald in his eight-page grandiloquent 1915 paean, "Spring Eternal."

Florid, overwrought, but true. The sun's gentle warmth did produce year-round crops. It began with grapes, but after the blight of 1886 killed thousands of vines in Orange, farmers planted tropical fruits, bananas, pineapples, and guavas … only to fail. By the 1890s, citrus was king. Groves of Valencia oranges, the sweet, juicy variety that originated somewhere on the Iberian Peninsula— no one is sure if they came from Portugal or Spain, although Columbus carried them to the New World in 1493, and it is said that the Spanish explorer Ponce de León planted them in Florida at the beginning of the sixteenth century—eventually carpeted the rich, loamy alluvial soils spreading from Santiago Creek. By 1948, a forest of five million Valencia orange trees grew on 67,000 acres in the county, roughly one hundred square miles of green.

Sunlight held this landscape in its incorporeal grasp. The sun illuminated the tight round canopies of dark leaves, highlighting their waxy yellow spears and the brownish-gray bark of the trunks. The sunlight spotlighted the almost perfectly spherical dangling orbs, converting them into innumerable glowing globes. The sunlight magnified the out-of-sync panorama of endless lush groves, cloaked in ripening fruit, set against the snow-dusted peaks of the San Gabriel Mountains.

And sunlight lit up the Santiago Orange Growers Association packinghouse, now the Sandi Simon Center for Dance, on North Cypress Street, a few blocks from the roundabout in Plaza Square, the bull's-eye from which the town of Orange emanates. This was Orange's first cooperative packinghouse, established in 1893, relocated to Cypress Street in 1918, along the tracks of the Atchison, Topeka & Santa Fe Railway (the indispensable farm-to-market transport monopoly). Daylight streamed into the one-and-one-half story building through twelve-light pivot windows, six-over-six double-hung windows, and a sawtooth roof with six rows of clerestory windows, ten feet high and 150 feet long.

Sawtooth industrial windows still serve their original purpose of allowing light to flood throughout the entire building.

A calculated cut through the original packinghouse's floor allows light to penetrate to lower levels.

Men harvested oranges, climbing three-legged ladders, snipping fruits from the trees, dropping them into long carrying sacks that were hauled by horse-drawn wagons (later trucks) to the Cypress Street packinghouse. Women, working beneath those north-facing sawtooths, ran the crops through a washer and air dryer, standing at conveyor belts, hand-sorting the fruit into three grades: top quality, average, and orchard run. These citrus workers, who had mostly emigrated from the central plateau states of Jalisco, Michoacán, and Zacatecas, Mexico, were paid abysmally low wages and lived in rented homes along and near Cypress Street.

The same sunlight that once grew so many oranges now illuminates dance studios.

Original, still-operable industrial clerestory windows are retrofit with actuators that open and expel heat as triggered by the contemporary mechanical system.

Finding a way to position the performance space in the center, as a two-story structure, while creating cuts to bring light and air to the lower level is the key strategy.

Polycarbonate walls allow light and views to permeate between studios and halls, breaking down distinctions between passersby and performers.

In 1929, 820,000 boxes (roughly 2,000 train carloads) were boxed at the Santiago Orange Growers Association's packinghouse, making it the world's largest shipper of oranges in its day. Fewer than twenty years later, Orange County's groves began slowly to disappear, yanked by the roots by men operating stump pullers to make way for the southward migration of Los Angeles's expanding population, hungry for suburban homes. A mysterious disease, too, swept through the groves, as the grape blight had decades before, and growers cashed out as developers offered magnificent prices for their rural acreage.

In 1965, the packinghouse was shuttered. The oranges of Orange had virtually disappeared. By 2022, commercial Valencia groves covered just seventy-six acres in all of Orange County. All that remained, really, was the sunlight. And the unintentional, unlikely crating depot that from 1918 had corralled light beneath a magnificent set of industrial windows. Cleaned, painted bright white, divided into a mezzanine and a ground floor, given a bending, baroque stairway and overlook, with rooms partitioned by glass and polycarbonate curtains and a sawtooth wooden wainscoting, it's a cathedral of natural light. With dancers in constant motion, as busy again throughout as when machinery hummed and rattled and the quick hands of workingwomen plucked thousands upon thousands of oranges from conveyors, piling them into boxes destined for cities nationwide.

FORMOSA 1140

→ P. 263

If you spend any time on the narrow, long north-south block of Formosa Avenue between Santa Monica Boulevard and Lexington Avenue, you'll begin to get a sense of a Los Angeles that isn't chronicled or cataloged or characterized. It's another *other* L.A., a road thirty-five feet wide—just wide enough for cars to park along each curbside and moving cars to squeeze by each other—comprised of the kind of sunshine that goes unnoticed. This isn't a spot where pellucid, crystalline light illuminates all that it touches. The light that falls here is inapposite: It won't intoxicate you, as it did the first generation of modernists to land in Los Angeles, compelling them to build homes meant to let it deep inside. It isn't the changeable light the phenomenological artists, like Robert Irwin with his Getty garden or James Turrell with his Skyspace observatories, set out to capture. The light along Formosa, and so many of the other nearby tiny streets built for Model T Fords and the lower ranks of production crews at the movie studios a few yards away, is eclipsed by the rest of L.A.'s garish glow. It isn't total darkness, though. It's penumbra.

By pushing the housing volume to one side of the lot, each residential unit is able to receive frontage on the public park, which is as integral to the lot as the building.

Perforated metal sheathing and fenestration of various sizes and orientations give the façade a choreographed rhythm.

Context is where you can find it. The color of the Formosa Cafe was the context we embraced. If you have a client who says, "We're going to find eleven people who will be happy to live in a red-and-orange building so don't worry about the color," you are in a good place.

Light that reaches the street is filtered through the mature canopies of sycamore, camphor, jacaranda, and ficus, which spread their branches above the sidewalks and, in places, meet over the centerline of the street. An L.A. allée of green and yellow and brown leaves, and mottled, woody limbs, marked by irregularly shaped patches of white or tan or basalt-black bark. The neighborhood operates on reflected, rather than overhead, light too. The two-story apartment buildings, one brick, the others wood-clad or stucco-skinned, project color faded by sun, weathered by rain, just as the sidewalks hold their castoff forms in irregular shapes that appear to the eye as black in the half-light but really are on the blue spectrum.

In short, nothing here on Formosa is pure. Not the light, and certainly not the buildings, which are a smattering of single-family, Spanish Revival, red-tiled houses, boxy pre-WWI apartments, dingbats built in the early 1960s, and contemporary three- and four-story behemoths with decorative balconies and stone veneers. The visual language of this street is, like the light, of an uncertain source, imprecise, without defining parameters—artistic or otherwise.

Why not, then, expand the palette, optically, orthographically, topographically, to become a freestanding building and an adjacent pocket park, open to the public? This dynamic patchwork of geometric blocks of red and orange perforated metal panels is its own radiating source of light; a scrim takes advantage of what light there is to cast complex shadows and shading on the actual building envelope of black, wooden paneling. The building shoots upward, taller than its neighbors, deepening the veiled light on the street but also bisecting the site along its length, freeing a third of the lot for use as a small pocket park—an unexpected patch of greenery and benches you encounter by chance as you might in dense Paris, as you wander. Or more likely, that you set out to visit it every day because this is your neighborhood and these are your sidewalks, your trees, your benches. And, your block.

Screens held away from the building's surface by the width of an exterior corridor at once provide strategic areas of privacy while maintaining an overall feel of openness and permeability.

GRANVILLE 1500

→ P. 264

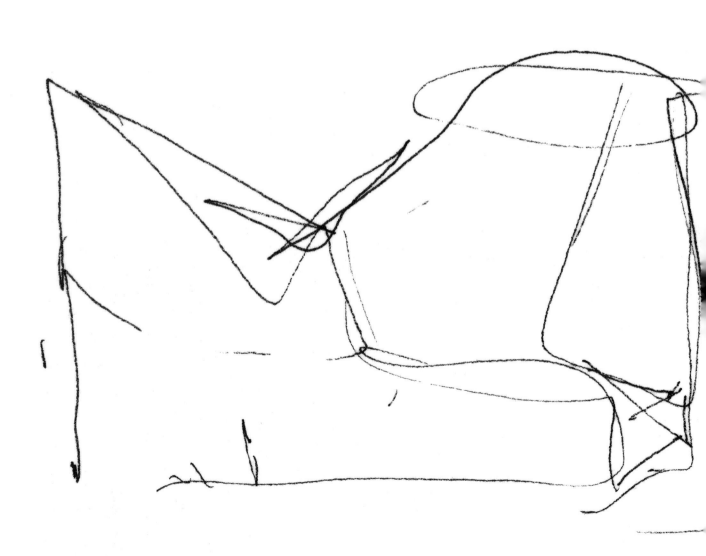

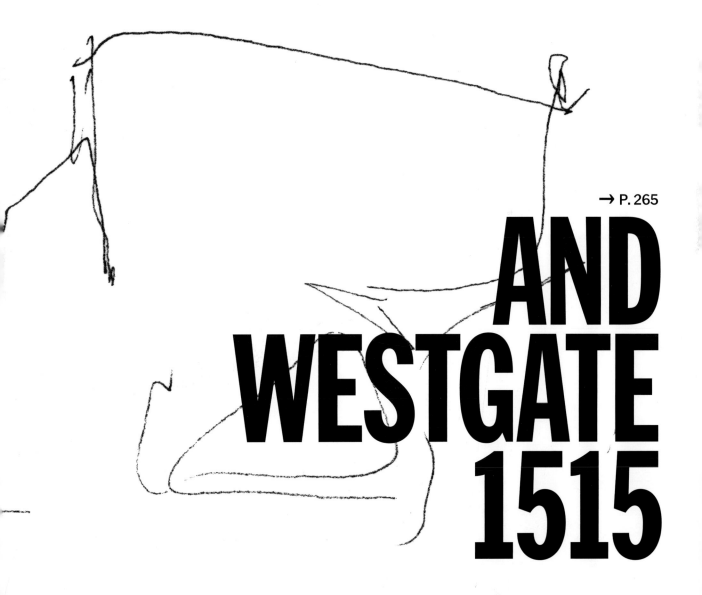

→ P. 265

AND WESTGATE 1515

Granville 1500, rather than being designed as one monolithic volume that would have exacerbated the impersonality of an already car-dominant Santa Monica Boulevard, is shaped into three discrete wedge-shaped segments that surround pedestrian-friendly spaces running the full depth of the lot.

Almost anywhere you are along Santa Monica Boulevard you can stop and take a slice, remove it, transport it a mile, two miles, ten miles, and, in the inexplicable and unknowable cosmology of Los Angeles, plop it down on another stretch of the same boulevard and it will sleeve in as if it had always been there. It stretches thirteen miles, from the eastern edge of Hollywood, beginning at Sunset Junction, to the Palisades, overlooking the Pacific Ocean. Laid out as a conduit for the Pacific Electric Railway cars, a route for rolling out the metropolis, Santa Monica Boulevard exudes a sense of journey. The intersecting and parallel street names tell part of the story: Iowa, Nebraska, Ohio, Idaho, Tennessee, Mississippi, Missouri, Texas, Montana, Pennsylvania, Colorado, Arizona, Rhode Island, Massachusetts, and Nevada (now Wilshire), reflect the westward pull of Manifest Destiny by denizens from elsewhere—it is no accident that Santa Monica Boulevard, which ends at the western lip of Los Angeles, is also the last leg of Route 66. You use Santa Monica Boulevard to *get somewhere*— which is why, for decades, it was shown on freeway builders' maps as an extension of the Hollywood Freeway.

So it is easy to accept the boulevard as everywhere and nowhere, a gloss on the weathered gibe that Los Angeles is seventy-two suburbs in search of a city. But then you notice an obscure asterisk posted on a street sign in the neighborhood, followed by: Kiowa Avenue. Kiowa means "the principal people" to the

Triangle-shaped cutouts at street level help to make the building feel as though it is lightly touching down on the ground rather than resting heavily upon it, while pragmatically increasing the width of sidewalks.

The language of folds and wedges that defines the exterior's personality continues in the interior spaces.

When you build in the city, you want to contribute back. You want to do something that's uplifting, interesting, and visually stimulating. It feels right.

Comanche, the Southern Plains tribe who occupied all the lands we now know as Midwestern states; and these state names today label the cross streets along Santa Monica Boulevard. But surely this anomalous insertion—chosen because it has that authoritative-sounding hard *K*—was never meant to concede the central truth about this stretch of Santa Monica Boulevard. Not 300 yards from the intersection of Westgate and Santa Monica is the Kuruvungna Springs, a natural source that once supported the Tongva village of the same name, which translates as "a place where we are in the sun." The springs have provided water to the native Tongva since at least the fifth century BCE and are still tended by the tribe, bubbling up some 25,000 gallons a day, but now relegated to a landmarked corner of University High School. Twenty-two centuries of continuous habitation had elapsed by the time Spanish explorers led by Gaspar de Portolá camped there in 1769. They described the settlement as a "good village" and reported receiving gifts of sage, watercress, chia, and fresh water. And, so, Santa Monica, indirectly, was named: Father Juan Crespí wrote that the flowing water reminded him of Saint Monica's tears, which she'd shed for her then-hedonistic son, the philosopher Augustine, before his conversion to Christianity. The city's founders, when told this story, were inspired to name it after the saint.

Directly across the street from Granville 1500, Westgate 1515 reveals a similar commitment to shaping social interaction by providing common outdoor spaces on every level and throughout the block.

Street-facing and interior-facing façades both share a commitment to outward-facing views, whether of Santa Monica Boulevard or inner courtyards, while community green spaces and an enhanced public plaza keep a dense, mixed-use site feeling like a civically engaged village.

The boulevard, then, begins a history of displacement. Spaniards accepted the Tongva's gifts, then enslaved them. Almost two hundred years later, the Japanese farmers, gardeners, and nurserymen who had since settled in the Sawtelle neighborhood were forcibly removed, their lands and homes and businesses forfeited during the internment of World War II. The specific evacuation order was Exclusion Order No. 8, which took in all the residents on Westgate and Granville Avenues. Strangely, twenty years before that, the independent city of Sawtelle itself was expropriated after Los Angeles police officers seized the city hall and its citizens were given the choice of running out of water or permitting themselves to be annexed to the burgeoning city with an overflowing aqueduct.

Santa Monica Boulevard was made to traverse this landscape; to allow you to speed through rather than pause. And the only real reason to pull over was to shop for ... a car. It was, and still is, dotted by automobile dealerships. Perhaps this was a hangover from the races the City of Santa Monica held from 1909 to 1919, when high-performance automobiles buzzed the streets, jackrabbiting through "Dead Man's Curve" (the treacherous corner of Wilshire and Ocean whose many wrecks lent the nickname Jan and Dean used in their 1963 teen drag racing hit tune). No surprise, then, that both the Granville and Westgate buildings are the immediate successors to a pair of car dealerships, razed to make way for a less transient, maybe more rooted and just, permanent habitation.

OBAMA BUILDING

→ P. 266

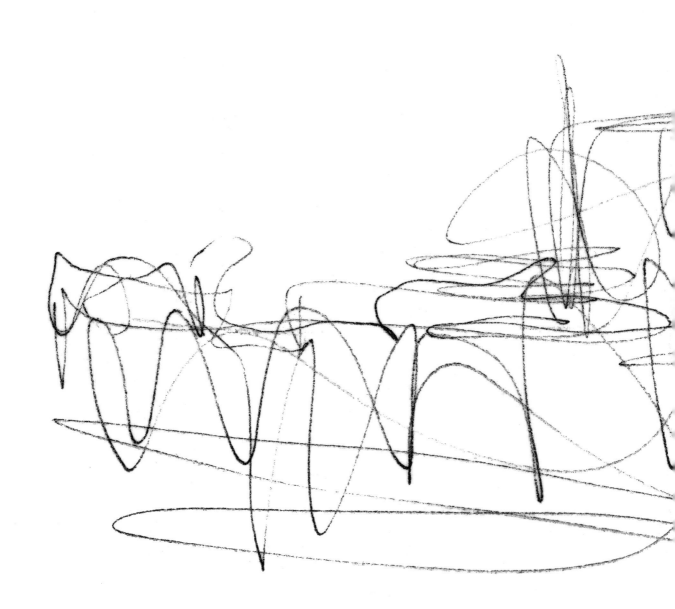

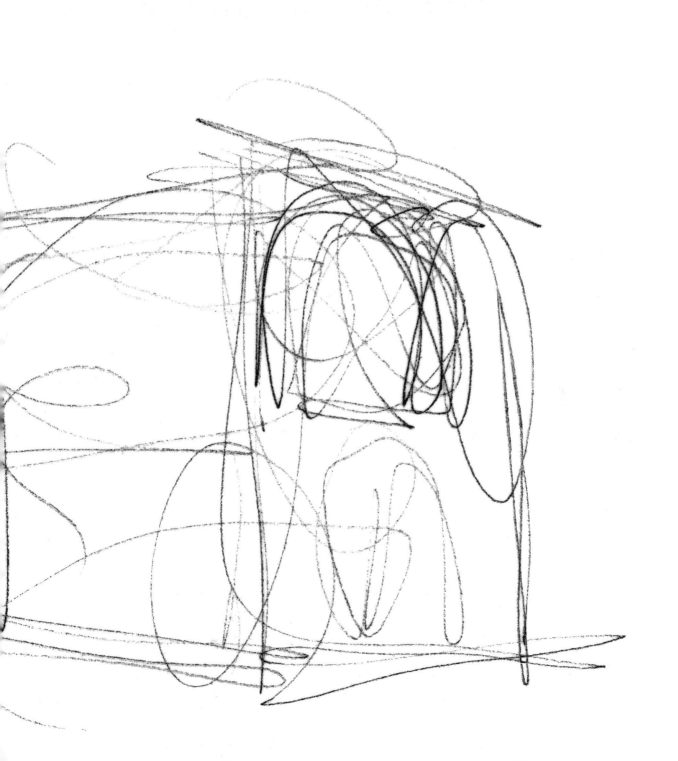

The inherent beauty of the original building's proportions remains, while new details allow for contemporary programming.

If you stand at the intersection of Grand River Avenue and Lahser Road, in Old Redford, it's likely you'll shortly be mesmerized by the steady stream of cars shuttling to and from Five Points and Seven Mile Road, in the vicinity of Redford Charter Township, and beyond, in the outer suburbs of Detroit. Some places are like that: inert, expressive of having been passed over. Overlookable. The dialectic goes like this: vital then, somnolent now. You sense this in the blank building façades, in the overly wide eight-lane expanse of Grand River, in the low, long, flat horizon, and the parcels of emptiness. It all spreads out inexorably, indistinguishable, an urban prairie. With so little distinctive to set eyes on, the visible becomes a blur.

Photos from the 1920s, '30s, '40s, and '50s prove that there *was* something to see here, then. Intense visual clutter dominated this crossroads of Redford. It was the vernacular of a small-town mercantile hub, awash in signage sticking out and up, the defining characteristic of the roadside environment. For one block or so northwest and southeast, along Grand River, and on a northbound stretch of Lahser, business after business advertised itself: Basch Diamonds, Kinsley's Drugs, Daly Jewelers, Elgin Watches, Miller's Feed and Seed, Nunn-Bush Shoes for Men, Awry Bakeries Buttercream Chocolate Pastry 3 for 10¢, Redford Bar-B-Q (offering billiards and snooker), Redford Lumber, Redford Theatre. The buildings recede, revert to functional boxes—some admittedly nicely detailed but prosaic against the kaleidoscope of uppercase sans serifs. Especially at night, when the electricity trickled the neon into efflorescence.

The most arresting view of Redford is of the former bank building at the corner of Grand River and Lahser sporting an erector-set pyramid of steel scaffolding holding aloft a massive billboard. The sign was clearly aimed at the motorcade of commuters. It was appended to the roof of a 1917 building whose architect, C. William Parker, knew exactly how to say "Bank." From its footings to its entablature it was textbook neoclassicism. Etched into its squared pediment was "Peoples State Bank of Redford." Sandwiched between two oversize Tuscan columns was a second-story arched window with a console (an S-shaped scroll bracket) as its keystone, and a pair of lanterns flanked the bank's solid oak doors. Pilasters separated the windows, and the cornices had dentils. The single unorthodox departure was a metal sign—harbinger of things to come— a stamped steel ribbon affixed to the parapet. Its embossed white letters spelled out "CAPITAL, SURPLUS & UNDIVIDED PROFITS - 160.000.00." Peoples Bank, the permanent sign implied, would always be offering "4% Interest on Savings." At the center of the sign a small granite acanthus wreath contained the traditional public-facing timepiece, a round clock with slender hands easily legible from sidewalk or street.

The vocabulary of the past will always identify the building as a former bank; the choice of a minimalist, black-and-white color palette for its rejuvenation indicates that it has a new purpose for the future and suggests itself as a literal blank canvas for the type of murals and street art that Detroit prizes.

Stepped storefront windows recommit the building to encouraging small business, foot traffic, and a hope that the area can regain its once-entrepreneurial energy.

It was a towering billboard, erected years later by Stein's Department Store, that began to erase the familiar financial imagery. That superstructure, remarkably, was at least one-and-one-half times the height of Peoples Bank, dwarfing the two-story building physically and visually. Attention drifted away from the bank as a signifier of commerce; the billboard took over that function. As that diadem aged and rusted, the building on which it stood was gradually stripped of its essential details. By 2005, the eighty-eight-year-old, 12,855-square-foot former bank building was abandoned, boarded up, its exterior so thoroughly denuded of ornamentation that it could have been a Styrofoam cutout.

A community center reanimates a space formerly left to decay.

And that flat, blank surface, which among its neighboring blocks as one of many such flat, blank surfaces, was subjected to a sort of artistic revanchism. Old Redford had long since become a Black area, and although it hadn't plunged into the kind of poverty experienced elsewhere in Detroit, it was still caught up in the decline and fall of the once-great city—and in the effort at resurrection. Local artists got out their paints and converted the board-ups into colorful canvases. The disused buildings along Grand River and Lahser became marquees, murals depicting a new narrative, from the lives of Malcolm X and Betty Shabazz to kids on an Archimedean teeter-totter propping up a young man watering flowers emerging from the decommissioned cooling tower of a nuclear reactor.

One mural—a painting, really—saved the crumbling Peoples State Bank building from condemnation. Chazz Miller painted Barack and Michelle Obama, in black tuxedo and white silk chiffon gown, respectively, in a loving embrace on the dance floor at the 2009 presidential inauguration. Soon after he painted *First Dance* directly above the sealed doorway, locals started calling the place the "Obama Building." Art magically transformed a relic into a beloved landmark.

The revived building adopts Miller's minimal color palette: black and white, and its purpose now is to allow artists to continue the tradition of turning blank walls into spaces for the display of art. Circuitously, we arrive at the beginning, again. The street corner is no longer overlookable. Its visual anchor is restored.

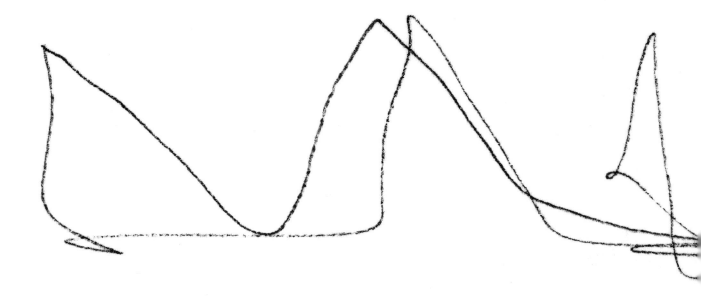

→ P. 267

SOUTH EAST8

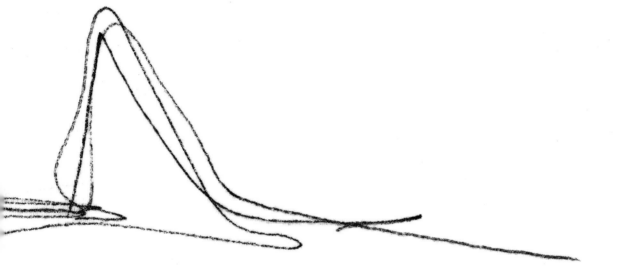

South East Street, Raleigh, is the southern stretch of East Street, which, until 1857, was the eastern boundary of this southern capital laid out by William Christmas in 1792. East Street, with North Street, South Street, and West Street, consist of the original 400 acres of the city, near the geographic center of North Carolina. These crisp, straight lines, surveyed along the cardinal points of the compass, did more than create a gridiron—a popular and useful form of eighteenth-century town planning Christmas borrowed from Savannah, Georgia, and Philadelphia, Pennsylvania. The quartet of streets outlining that tidy quadrangle, which after 1857 was expanded to a neat square mile, were more than city limits. They were color lines, psychic and physical barriers demarcating separation of the races, perhaps even more so when the long, dark epoch of slavery became the long, dark epoch of Jim Crow, robbing freed slaves of true emancipation. South East Street was one of the barriers that sealed Raleigh proper from its Black inhabitants.

The heritage of the fourteen blocks of that one street runs deep into the founding sin of the nation. Not a half mile from South East Street, in antebellum North Carolina, free Blacks had been stripped by the state legislature—meeting in the Capitol Building in Capitol Square in Raleigh—of the right to vote, preach, carry firearms, marry whites or slaves, or even to transact business with slaves. They could, however, live and own land inside the city, but Raleigh's growing free Black citizenry were, in the main, clustered outside the city limits, on cheap tracts of bottomland near the railroads where they worked. These outlying areas were disdained by the city's powerful white elites as "the suburbs," occupied by "indolent and worthless [free blacks] living not by labor but by depredation and by midnight robberies."

Building geometry, while distinctive, integrates seamlessly into the neighborhood.

What was de facto became de jure in the decades after the Civil War. Freed slaves were forbidden by racist deed covenants and open segregation from buying or renting in Raleigh. And, so, those old borders became the edges of not-quite-exclusively Black neighborhoods. None more so than South East Street, beyond whose centerline a number of "freeman's villages" were situated.

These became neighborhoods built on small lots, some only twenty-five feet wide, on narrow streets. Lining them were shotgun cottages, typically one room wide by three rooms deep, with a front porch; two-room dwellings with center gables; and saddlebag houses, two separate rooms with two front entries and a shared central chimney. These were the homes of the working poor, and so they largely remained into the 1990s—although often improved and expanded, somewhat, yet still lower-class, Black owned, largely segregated. Dotted throughout were the more elegant homes of the doctors, lawyers, dentists, shopkeepers, and businessmen, whose lives and homes were bound to the

lives and homes of their less-prosperous neighbors. With them grew up a thriving Black main street—East Hargett Street—full of Black churches, Black schools, Black identity and camaraderie.

The 300 block of South East Street was one part of this wider place: a group of simple, gable-front, one-story wooden houses, which by the late 1950s included Smith Temple Free Will Baptist Church, a modest, working-class church founded in 1944. A plain building of bricks and mortar and a white steeple. At some point, one house was replaced by a little concrete bunker, occupied by a welding firm. A wholesale grocery warehouse also went up, and a printer's shop was appended to a tiny shingled house fronted by a porch protected by an uncertain shed roof. Still, the street persisted, largely as is, as was, residing in a settled, if not always easy, apartness from the core of the city only eight blocks away.

Then something happened to South East Street—and as continues to happen to other streets in Southeast Raleigh. Several of the old, modest homes were bought, razed, replaced. Not that you'd know it just by looking. The houses that popped up almost uniformly shared the uncomplicated design of their predecessors: four walls beneath a pitched roof, with gables at either end, and a porch held up with simple posts, facing the street. Only now they had two stories, not one. Even the muted greens, grays, and yellows seemed applied with an old brush. This gentrification began in the late 1990s, and felt as if the new homes had been extruded from those dating back to the previous century.

Thus, 323 South East Street. It's a riff on a riff: a two-story, primary-color box with conjoined pitched roofs ski-slope steep, falling away from one another at raked angles. Like the cookie-cutter developer vernacular occupying much of the rest of the block, the duplex "fits in" by seeming to adopt the local jargon—only to wrench it beyond the angle of repose. South East Street, too, has been wrenched, the racial geography cemented into the street turned on its head as poorer Blacks move out and better-off whites move in. "Plus ça change, plus c'est la même chose."

The new roofline's form is rooted in its context.

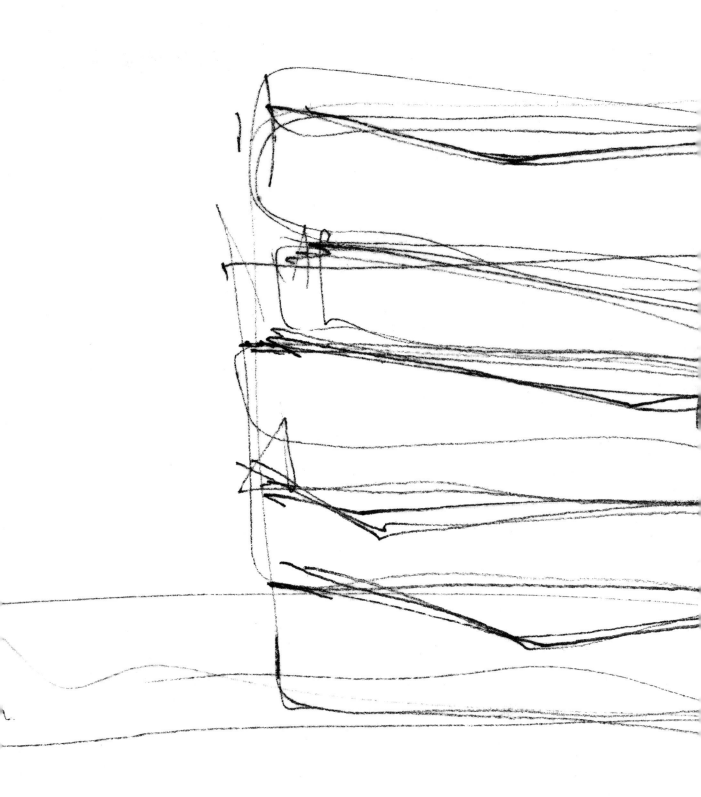

SYCAMORE 953

→ P. 268

Three superficially disparate facts present themselves when you're standing at the corner of Sycamore and Romaine, in the heart of industrial Hollywood. First, that there was, and remains, an industrial Hollywood. A place where the illusions of the movies were—and still are—mostly handcrafted. It is no accident that Hollywood calls itself "the industry," or that the term alludes to manufacturing. Films might be an art form, but they're impossible without carpentry and machine shops, technical geniuses lapping steel and optical glass and toying with tungsten, silver nitrate, copper wire, celluloid, shellac, and vinyl, pressing and sewing fabric, making cosmetics, and dry-cleaning wardrobe. Walk about half a mile in any direction from this corner and you'll run into the places where Kodak made film, Technicolor processed it, RCA and Decca recorded its sound, Mole-Richardson developed incandescent lighting for its sets, and a seventeen-year-old, C. Dodge Dunning, invented the blue screen traveling matte shot—the "Dunning Process," eventually shortened to "process shot"—which made it possible for King Kong to climb the Empire State Building just twenty-two months after it had conquered the Manhattan skyline.

Less visible to the naked eye, yet standing just sixty feet away, directly across Sycamore, is a building that completely embodies the underbelly of Hollywood— the tyrannical personalities, the sexual escapades, the paranoia, the drive for absolute power, the descent into madness. Here, in just ninety days in 1930, Howard Hughes, the daredevil aviator and wealthy son of a Texas tool and die maker, built his color film manufacturing plant … three decades before color films would become financially feasible and consign black and white to the vaults. Here, with the might of an actual industrial enterprise behind him, he became a mogul, produced movies, dated stars (most famously Katharine Hepburn), personally edited the film. Here, he expanded his industrial empire, converting the building to produce "jamless" bullet belts that could feed cartridges at a rate of 840 rounds per minute for fighter planes and bomber machine guns during World War II, then shifting to control TV stations, airlines, hotels, and much of Las Vegas, all while building satellites and missiles for the Pentagon. Here, his industrial domain collapsed though he finished a billionaire (when that meant something), and he became the world's richest recluse, obsessively secretive, compulsively scrubbing clean everything he touched, an insomniac glued to a television station broadcasting old movies at his command.

Floors currently allocated to parking are designed to be converted to office space in the future, as needed, with minimal intervention.

Thin concrete plates act as shades to control sunlight penetration to the office interiors while establishing a consistent visual language that accentuates how the building shifts and cantilevers, while floor-to-ceiling height increases incrementally on topmost levels, maximizing views.

The most obvious landmark at this corner is unavoidably, clamorously in plain sight: the Cemex Concrete Plant. Concrete was first mixed at Sycamore and Romaine in 1923, when highway builders W. L. Stine and J. Russell Ellis opened the state's first cement mixing plant on the dirt parcel where the only nearby structures were an ice machinery and storage facility and a distilled water manufacturer. From that year on, cement trucks have been swinging their elephant torsos into the graveled driveway and awaiting their ten-cubic-yard batch of the material that, it seems likely, paved every street in the area and supplied all 6,750 barrels of cement used for Hughes's Multicolor Limited building, and the innumerable reinforced, fireproof concrete buildings Hollywood constructed to make movies.

It was a somewhat distressed area and lacked pedestrian life. To be a part of the team bringing urban renewal was immensely important. The street and sidewalk came alive again.

By inserting street-level retail between underground and second-through-fifth-floor parking, the building participates in encouraging a return of foot traffic to the neighborhood.

With its steep conveyor tower, giant hoppers, and shantytown-style office on stilts, Cemex—still called Transit Mixed by those who've been in the neighborhood a while—looks like a collage of sheet metal scraps. Or a solitary centurion posted guard over a territory whose character was once defined by over 750 entertainment-related industrial and commercial properties. More than a relict or vestige, it is the stubborn muse of a melody played for over a hundred years now: continuously mixing sand, crushed rock, water, and Portland cement. Yard after cubic yard emerges, the liquid-become-solid that can be molded into almost any structural form—walls and foundations and floors and pavements. We live in a postindustrial age, governed by zeros and ones producing ephemeral experiences rather than palpable objects, yet the armature of our world is, contradictorily, fashioned from the same raw material Hadrian used to build the Pantheon in second-century Rome.

Sycamore 953 hovers between the solidified, yet ever-changing, world simmering in the reinforced concrete structures that are its closest neighbors and the immutable factory ceaselessly churning slurry across the roadway. Unprepossessing like its surroundings—even those that have already been gentrified, face-lifted, and repurposed—it tells you almost nothing of what transpires within. Because it requires no legibility, it might seem inscrutable. But, really, the seeming anonymity is a mask for modesty. The building eschews overstatement and subtly, in sotto voce, speaks to the expressive quality of concrete. You can't help but notice how ultrathin the concrete floor plates seem, even as they jut out and support chevrons of floor-to-ceiling glass walls. The concrete will age, it will change color, its mood will adapt to sunlight and shadow. That's all.

Twists and steps in the building's volume create terraces and ledges.

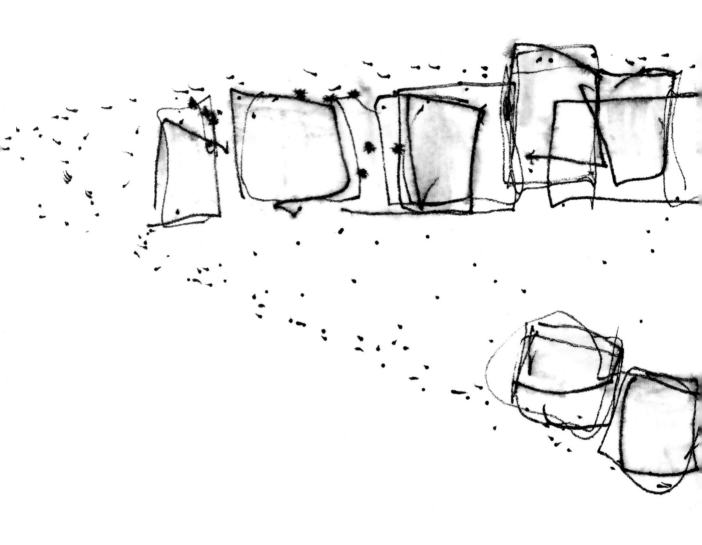

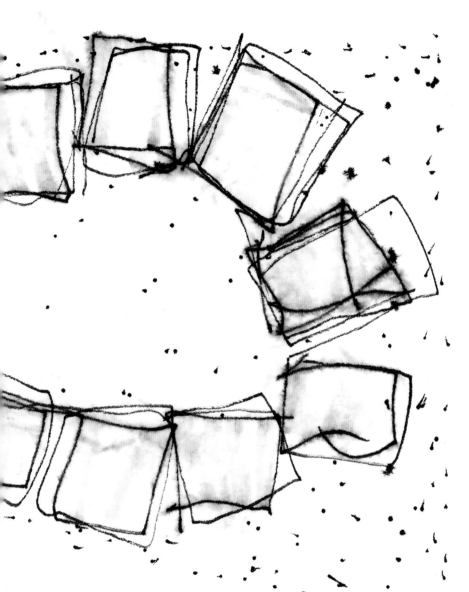

→ P. 269

ISLA INTERSECTIONS

Situated within close proximity to one of the world's busiest freeway interchanges, the meeting of the 110 and 105 freeways, the design works to make a challenging location livable.

SOMEWHERE is HERE.

First impressions: 283 West Imperial Highway, an address that did not exist until 2019, lies at an intersection of three streets: Broadway, Athens, Imperial Highway. A fragment marooned where the city stopped. A two-dimensional reliquary for the visible and invisible fallout of time and circumstance and amnesia. One look at the place might convince you of the necessary balm of forgetting and the seduction of willful oblivion. What's here? A triangle nine miles south of City Hall, paved as flat and inert as a granite tabletop: nothing moves, nothing grows. The gray pavement, terminating at the north end in a nosecone, an inanimate artifact persevering between streets, beneath freeway interchanges towering 130 feet above.

Where are we? What kind of foundation is this? Where is the bedrock? Can we build in emptiness so full of the unknown?

Here's what we know: 283 Imperial Highway was not on the map, until it was. The spit exists but not as the tiny, city-owned parcel where we'll build. It starts off in the middle of railroad tracks, literally, the by-product of tracts and subdivisions from when the Spanish ranchos were being sold piece by piece to land speculators and Los Angeles was in the business of annexation. The city headed south, grabbing the port at San Pedro, and with it pieces of land to either side of the Shoestring Strip addition that connected downtown to the coveted port. As-yet-nonexistent 283 was swept into the Green Meadows addition, in 1926, which ate up the Moneta tract, Athens-on-the-Hill, Athens Acres, Athens itself. Which, for starters, explains one part of the triangle-to-be: Athens Way was once the intended main street of a speculator's dreamed-up, fanciful suburb, imbued with the Platonic ideal borrowed from the city-state. Maps tell the story. The Los Angeles Railway pushed south, heading along Broadway, terminating at Athens Way and 116th Street—three blocks below our site. Broadway was called Moneta Avenue until 113th Street, where it trickled off at a slight easterly angle to become a narrow tributary, while Athens Way became the streetcar route. The yellow cars ran down an eighty-foot-wide dirt median, and Athens was a street divided by trolley car tracks. Imperial Highway, too, existed, but went by the name Monte Vista Avenue, and 113th was called Goss Avenue.

The project took cues from local residents' values by embracing artistry and social equity. It is designed to create space where people will want to spend time engaging with each other and engaging the community at large—something the site discouraged before construction.

The railway median defined the spot. Athens, and the streetcars, went straight, Broadway veered off. In 1935 a corner was rounded over and shaved into a radius, but still until the late 1940s, when gas-powered buses replaced electric trolleys, there was no triangle. And then, it appeared. The railway right-of-way fell into desuetude, Broadway swallowed most of it, ballooning to a boulevard two hundred feet across. Now Athens Way was the tributary, and the island bounded by the three streets appeared, 17,384 square feet of … palimpsest, pentimento, palindrome.

Our site resonated with things written, scratched off, rewritten; painted, painted over; run forward, run backward. You could read this continuity, or discontinuity, in two footnotes, and in the defining epic narrative towering above—the construction of the Harbor Freeway, begun in 1954, then called the Century Freeway, inaugurated in 1982. Twice the triangle became the subject of civic interest. First, on March 31, 1949, at the request of Post No. 488 of the American Legion, the city council approved a monument on the traffic island to those who gave their lives in World War II. Fifteen years later, on May 13, 1964, the council entertained a memorial to Carl Hoffman, the founder of the Imperial Highway Association and "the man most responsible for the completion of the Imperial Highway from the mountains to the sea."

The first memorial seemed natural. The war had ended and building a monument to fallen soldiers on a city-owned plot aligned with an age-old tradition. The second was a bit more obscure. Few recalled the origins of the street. The "Imperial" referred to the Imperial Valley, rich agricultural land on the Mexican border. Los Angeles had plotted for decades to run a 215-mile highway from Brawley in the melon-growing valley to meet the sea at El Segundo. Imperial was apt, "Athens" too. The grandiose ambitions of the owners of the surrounding alfalfa acres were inscribed in those names, echoes of the empires

This, to me, represents what it's like to build in Los Angeles. This project's DNA is utilitarian. It's authentic and represents a solution that is married to where it's at. There's intensity, grittiness, ruggedness.

A reduced roofline strengthens the connection between the building and the Annenberg Paseo, which runs between the project and a stretch of freeway interchange, creating a "slow space" that gives preference to pedestrians and bikers along the west side of the site.

of the ancient world. (Look no further than nearby Laconia, Olympia, and Ionia streets, for direct reference to Hellenic Greece.) They built the empires, in a way, by drilling a mile deep into the tar-sand lands, pumping oil—so much oil that each year enough was siphoned that it could have filled a river forty-four feet wide, one foot deep, and 3,065 miles long, or from Los Angeles to New York. The father of the notorious skinflint industrialist and billionaire J. Paul Getty was a pioneering oilman who operated at least four wells in Athens township; one he named for the mythical figure Hercules. With the money he inherited, Getty the son built a mansion modeled on the Roman Villa dei Papyri in Herculaneum, Italy. So it goes.

Then they built the Century Freeway, the final leg of the hoped-for Imperial Highway, which shredded 8,000 homes immediately south, parallel to the street once called Monte Vista. Twenty-five thousand working-class residents living in the corridor were forced out; left behind was a clear-swept swath of land stretching block after block, as if a conquering army had marched through. In 1965, the same year the California Highway Commission adopted the slash-and-burn route for the Century Freeway, it approved the Beverly Hills Freeway. "Community controversies" followed these announcements, but only one freeway went from being a line on the map to a concrete ribbon through the heart of a neighborhood. An echo, surely, of an imperial power imposing its will; a monument in concrete durable enough to outlive the memory of the disrupted lives and the short-circuited streets and, especially, the streetcar that had run along Athens Way.

Even the horizon was obliterated. From that tiny patch at Athens and Broadway and 113th, the view south is of an incomprehensively massive structure, composed of thirty-four road beds where the Harbor Freeway and the Century Freeway overlap and intersect. From above, it appears as if an Iron Cross has been drawn onto the landscape, by the hand of a cartographer whose job it was to make sense out of a nebula but could not. In two minutes, you can walk across Imperial Highway and be standing under this sublime beast, cut off irrevocably from the rest of the world. Is this spot a titanic, three-dimensional extrusion of the tiny, flat abandoned site across the street?

Thus, Islas. Our buildings occupy the edges of this uneasy, uncertain, undefined plot. They don't square up, they don't form a perfect line or wall, they tiptoe in a deferential gait. It makes sense that the first buildings to appear on that triangle are liminal. They cross both sides of the boundary or threshold between past and future, present and absent, placeless and place.

DILLON 617

→ P. 270

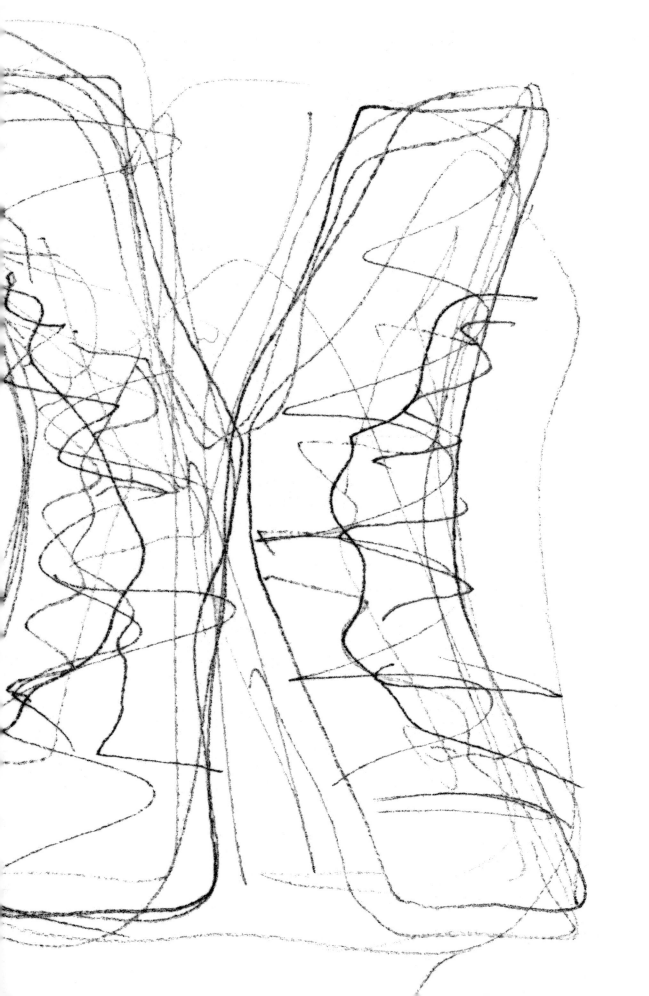

If geography is destiny, cartography is our certain fate, even more so. In 1850, when California was admitted to the union, Los Angeles, the Spanish pueblo founded in 1781, became an Anglo outpost on the lip of the almost-completed continental United States. That year, the city incorporated itself, marking as its own western edge the street now called Hoover. Army Lieutenant Edward O.C. Ord was paid $3,000 to lay out the city streets and, although he only mapped a small piece of the original four square leagues (about twenty-five square miles) granted to the pueblo by the Spanish crown, the streets and city lots he platted followed the cardinal points of the compass. Ord's once and future Los Angeles—today's downtown was nearly synonymous for the whole of Los Angeles in the 1850s—was laid out on a true north-south path, parallel to then-existing South Main Street. But the Spanish town followed North Main Street, falling approximately 36 degrees east of true north; as the city expanded westward, it followed this slightly askew trajectory. And then something else happened. Those original pueblo lines were abandoned in favor of Ord's, beginning at Hoover Street and marching west. Thereby, Los Angeles became a city on two grids.

Which is where the intersection of Dillon Street, Silver Lake Boulevard, and Bellevue Avenue come in. The tripartite meeting of roadways marks essentially where the two grids collide. Bellevue Avenue to one side, steadfast and defiant, running straight and true from its beginnings at Figueroa, downtown, to its end at Hoover, in east Hollywood. But its path emanates from the sixteenth-century Spanish Law of the Indies, which decreed that the streets and house lots in the cities of New Spain follow a 45-degree orientation from true north-south. That way, the low-slung houses would catch equal amounts of sunlight on all sides throughout the day. Despite the royal mandate, L.A. could only realistically achieve a 36-degree slant because of the city's original spine, the notoriously fickle and flood-prone Los Angeles River. This made an awkward conjoining with Ord's map that much more inevitable. Two worlds straddle nearly the same space.

Two long bars span the length of the block, connected in between by exterior walkways, while balconies punched and set back into the façade at alternating intervals ensure each unit has access to outdoor space.

Not surprisingly, this rough, overlapping border produces dualities. Silver Lake, the neighborhood where Dillon Street runs, is itself Janus-like. The upper reaches, around the reservoir, have a circulation plan that follows natural hillside topography in an intuitive and aesthically pleasing way. It attracted artists and dancers and musicians and writers, political refugees and dissidents, and, famously, architects. Frank Lloyd Wright, Rudolph Schindler, Richard Neutra, Gregory Ain, John Lautner, and Raphael Soriano all built there. Anaïs Nin wrote her erotic short stories and diaries in a house designed by Eric Lloyd Wright; Ain's Avenel Co-Op was deemed by the House Un-American Activities Committee "a cooperative living experiment for a group of communists" during the McCarthy-era witch hunts. The streets about a mile south, however, house another, decidedly earthbound sphere altogether. As Silver Lake Boulevard curves beneath the Hollywood Freeway, just a few yards down the road from Dillon and Bellevue, it disappears into a maze of asphalt that seems almost as if it was designed to confound, to prevent escape: Temple, Virgil, Smilax, Beverly, and Westmoreland converge as a sequence of twisting lines in search of open road. The dual grids come to outright blows here. Could it be a coincidence that this southern tip of Silver Lake has remained tough, poor, and working class? No midcentury cultural heritage sites or brand-name authors here; it is almost the polar opposite, in spirit, to its doppelgänger namesake. It's the kind of place where, for two generations, the local landmark was Phil's Transfer and Storage, a warehouse and parking lot for moving vans that occupied a former Thrifty Mart corner store—abandoned after neighborhood kids looted the place following a devasting fire in 1964.

When you tell clients that a black building is the correct solution, their initial instinct is to say, "That's not very welcoming." But I do believe they were excited in the end.

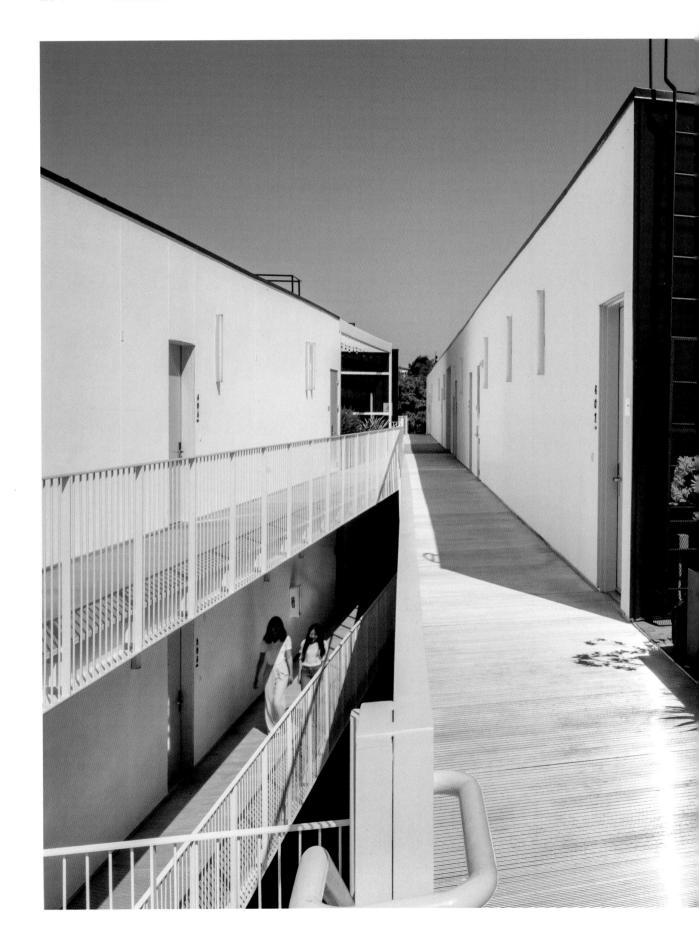

A commitment to park spaces within and around the building continues at roof level.

Still, that underlying tension generates possibilities, and complexities. When Dillon 617 was first conceived, it was meant to be one building, spanning the old Phil's Transfer site and an empty lot next door. But the neighborhood was incensed with the idea of the massing one large building would add, and, battling the developer, forced a bifurcation. Two buildings emerged where one had been intended. One was clad entirely in black, the other entirely in white. As if the map really could dictate destiny, Dillon 617 was pushed across two back-to-back lots and became a building with two front doors—one facing east, one facing west. And right down the middle, the building split open, two halves converging to form an oblique wedge, as if the acute angles of the nearby streets had been traced onto a piece of vellum and overlaid neatly onto the site. One can sense that this, indeed, is the cartographer's hand still at work.

Where the building's two volumes meet at the K-shaped "pinch point," residents also have the chance to meet and interact.

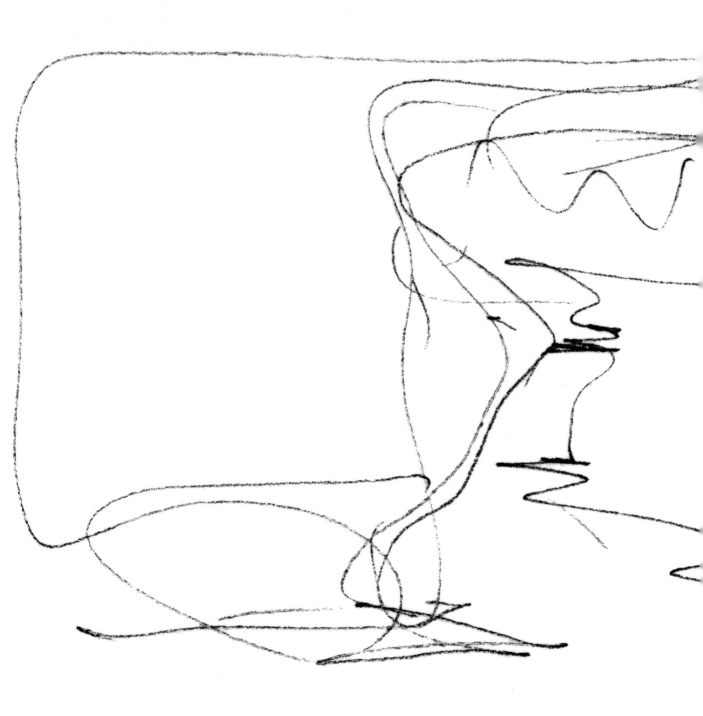

SAN VICENTE 935

→ P. 271

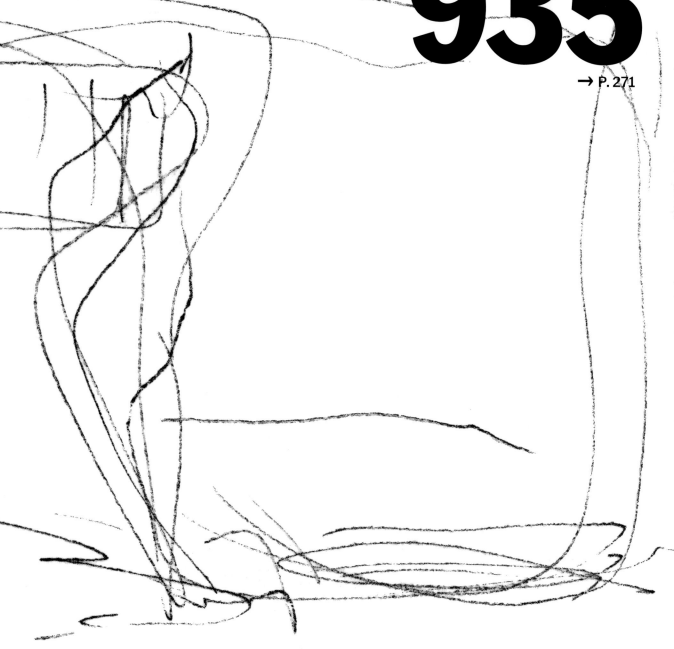

An aerial shot of North San Vicente Boulevard, taken in 1961, shows the entire block from Santa Monica Boulevard to Sunset lined by tiny houses. Subtle differences distinguished plains cottages from bungalows, but they were all examples of vernacular at the turn of the twentieth century: hipped roofs, narrow wooden clapboard siding, simple end boards and window trim, extended eaves that were either boxed or had decorative brackets. Porches, too, and on occasion, columns. When they were built, San Vicente was Clark Avenue, named for and by the co-owner of the 5.5-acre town of Sherman on land adjacent to the new electric streetcar line owned by Eli P. Clark and his partner, Moses Hazeltine Sherman. Sherman's name was appended to the main street— later renamed Santa Monica Boulevard—and to the railway service facility they built at the halfway point along the "Balloon Line" route, which made a circuit between Los Angeles and Santa Monica. By 1910, their Los Angeles Pacific Railway facility had four enormous brick buildings: a car barn, milling and car-building shops, electrical substation and boiler room, and an office building. There was also a wood-frame car barn, brass foundry, pattern shop (where wooden molds for the foundry were made), and nine other buildings.

Fully a quarter of the main elevation facing San Vicente is carved out to provide visual and physical connection between street and internal courtyard.

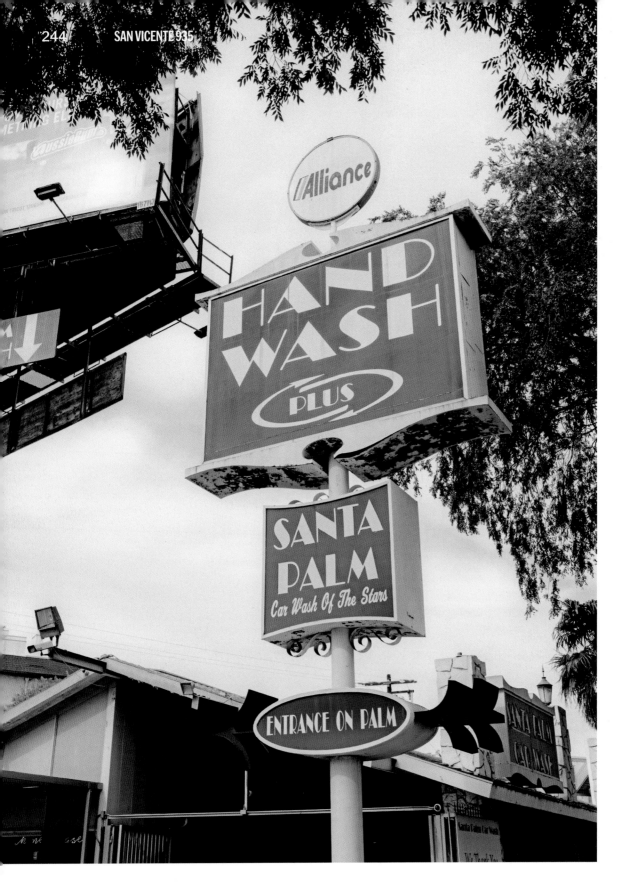

935

White, specially developed powder-coated fiber cement board made of recycled content contrasts richly with locally sourced and forest-managed wood that finds purpose as both cladding and shading.

The town of Sherman grew around the rail yards, with simple, inexpensive houses occupied by railway workers, mostly immigrant men without families who lent the area its reputation as a rough-and-tumble company town. One by one, the bungalows got picked off. By 1953, when the last streetcar made its run on Santa Monica Boulevard, West Hollywood was built out, and a wave of redevelopment ensued. The new vernacular "stucco box," aka the multifamily dingbat apartment building—named for the midcentury starburst ornaments adorning the stucco façades—replaced the modest single-family houses. Occupying the entirety of its parcel, typically employing tuck-under parking to accommodate cars, this rectangular, two-story building would be most often clad in pastel shades of stucco, with wooden flourishes, sometimes in the form of wide horizontal shingles or fascia boards, and with a fanciful name affixed in wooden or metal scrollwork lettering. A perforated metal gate— almost never locked—completed the portrait.

This was definitely a by-product of incentives. When we designed it, the key was to get the city to approve a very limited courtyard. We met the minimum requirements, but we activated the open space we had by bringing in the circulation.

Circulation for all four stories, including the primary exterior sculptural stair, is set within the common courtyard.

Unexpectedly shaped portals in the shutters direct views.

All units feature exposures on three sides, allowing ample light.

935 North was a lonely holdout. By 1987, it was one of only two bungalows left on that block of San Vicente, above the dogleg where the street straightens out at Cynthia Avenue before its final climb to Sunset Boulevard—and where San Vicente reverts to its original name, Clark Street. In 1999, the City of West Hollywood deemed 935 too ramshackle and defaced to be worthy of historic preservation; thirteen years later, it was demolished, making way for only the second building to occupy the narrow site in its 120 years of platted existence.

Eerie how the new enfolds the vernacular of the old. The unpretentious bungalow was loved for the magical versatility of basic materials and forms. Pitched roofs could be pitched to different slopes; eaves could be deepened or shallowed; porches projected or recessed; rafters carved or left plain; gables emboldened with decorative shingles or pierced with wooden pickets to form vents. With an economy of metal, wood, and cement board, 935 achieves a similarly nimble kaleidoscope. Wooden slats, neat and straight, begin to bulge and bend like old clapboard siding given a new life in a new century. A folding shutter— so utterly practical on a hot summer day—projects like a newfangled eave. A single column supports interlocking volumes, forming an enormous porch. Taut stainless-steel wires incise endlessly changing webs of shadow, decorative "shingles" cast in light, not wood. Entirely different, the now-vanished bungalow and its replacement four-story apartment. The earlier, relaxed, maybe even sedentary, and altogether comforting. The later, more urgent, energetic, swift. Yet, in the freedom to manipulate the glossary of materials to produce multiple effects without resorting to gimmick or trope, much alike.

PROJECT CREDITS

CANYON5

P. 14 ←

LOCATION: Los Angeles, California
SIZE: 12,000 SF
PROGRAM: 5 Small Lot Subdivision Homes
COMPLETION: 2021
ARCHITECT: Lorcan O'Herlihy Architects [LOHA]
CLIENT: Leeor Maciborski
PHOTOGRAPHER: Here and Now Agency
PRINCIPAL-IN-CHARGE: Lorcan O'Herlihy
PROJECT DIRECTOR: Brian Adolph
PROJECT LEADS: Noelle White, Nick Hopson
PROJECT ASSIST: Chris Gassaway, Cameron Overy, Leo Yu
OWNER: Leeor Maciborski

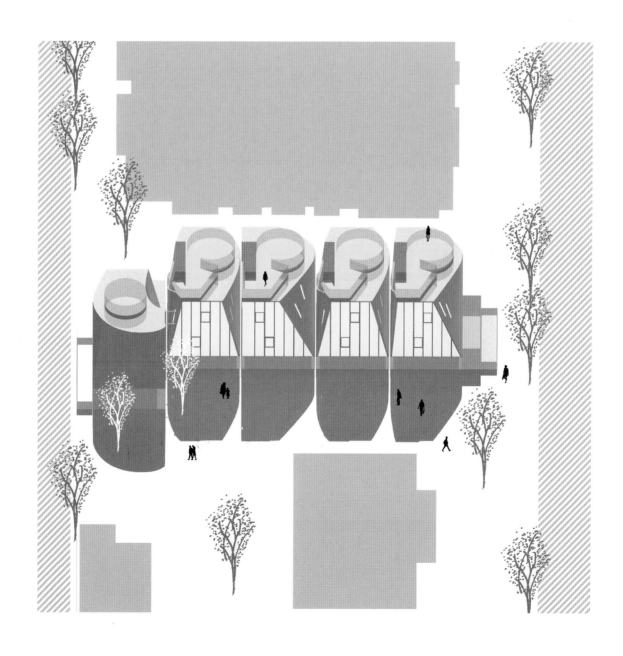

MLK1101 SUPPORTIVE HOUSING

P. 30 ←

LOCATION: Los Angeles, California
SIZE: 34,000 SF with 4,000 SF Park Space
PROGRAM: 26-Unit Affordable Housing with Street-Level
Community Space, Supportive Services,
and Community Garden
COMPLETION: 2019
ARCHITECT: Lorcan O'Herlihy Architects [LOHA]
CLIENT: Holos Communities
PHOTOGRAPHER: Here and Now Agency
PRINCIPAL-IN-CHARGE: Lorcan O'Herlihy
PROJECT DIRECTOR: Brian Adolph, Nick Hopson
PROJECT LEADS: Dana Lydon, Santiago Tolosa
PROJECT TEAM: Chris Gassaway, Ghazal Khezri,
Christopher Lim
OWNER: Holos Communities

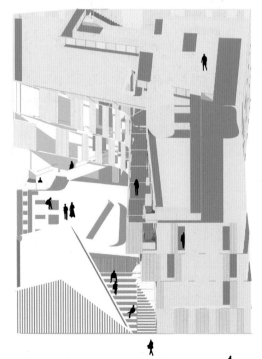

BRUSH PARK

P. 44 ←

LOCATION: Detroit, Michigan
SIZE: 210,000 SF
PROGRAM: 4 Mixed-Use Buildings with 134-Unit Housing and Ground Floor Retail
COMPLETION: 2022
ARCHITECT: Lorcan O'Herlihy Architects [LOHA]
CLIENT: Bedrock Detroit
PHOTOGRAPHER: Jason Keen
PRINCIPAL-IN-CHARGE: Lorcan O'Herlihy
PROJECT LEADS: Noelle White, Matthew Biglin
PROJECT TEAM: Ryan Caldera, Nick Hopson, Nicholas Muraglia, Cameron Overy, Lucia Sanchez-Ramirez, Lyannie Tran
PROJECT ASSIST: Anna Hermann
OWNER: Bedrock Detroit

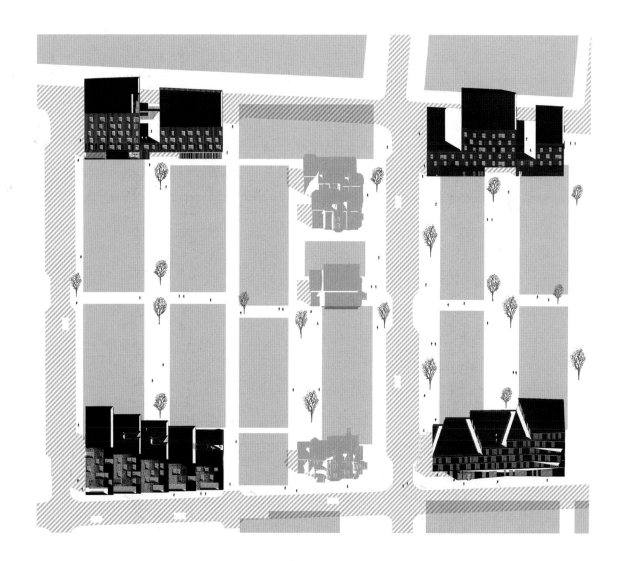

UCSB SAN JOAQUIN STUDENT HOUSING

P. 64 ←

LOCATION: Santa Barbara, California
SIZE: 95,000 SF
PROGRAM: University Student Housing with Study Rooms, Lounges, Kitchens, and Ancillary Spaces
COMPLETION: 2017
ARCHITECT: Lorcan O'Herlihy Architects [LOHA]
CLIENT: University of California, Santa Barbara
PHOTOGRAPHER: Bruce Damonte
PRINCIPAL-IN-CHARGE: Lorcan O'Herlihy
PROJECT DIRECTOR: Donnie Schmidt
PROJECT LEAD: Damian Possidente
PROJECT TEAM: Tang Chuenchomphu, Jessica Colangelo, Noelle White
OWNER: University of California, Santa Barbara

WILLOUGHBY 7917

P. 80 ←

LOCATION: West Hollywood, California
SIZE: 24,000 SF
PROGRAM: 8-Unit Multi-Family Housing
COMPLETION: 2008
ARCHITECT: Lorcan O'Herlihy Architects [LOHA]
CLIENT: Whitecap Development, LLC
PHOTOGRAPHERS: Lawrence Anderson, Tate Lown
PRINCIPAL-IN-CHARGE: Lorcan O'Herlihy
PROJECT LEAD: Pierre De Angelis
PROJECT TEAM: Sabrina Schmidt-Wetekam,
Alex Morassut
OWNER: Whitecap Development, LLC

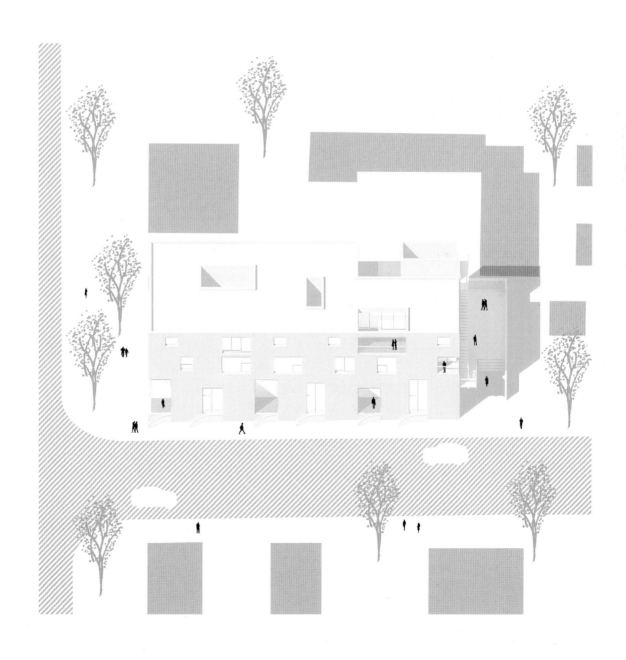

CLOVERDALE 749

P. 96 ←

LOCATION: Los Angeles, California
SIZE: 10,500 SF
PROGRAM: 6-Unit Housing
COMPLETION: 2015
ARCHITECT: Lorcan O'Herlihy Architects [LOHA]
CLIENT: Papalian Capital Partners
PHOTOGRAPHER: Lawrence Anderson
PRINCIPAL-IN-CHARGE: Lorcan O'Herlihy
PROJECT DIRECTOR: Donnie Schmidt
PROJECT LEAD: Alex Morassut
PROJECT TEAM: Dana Lydon
OWNER: Papalian Capital Partners

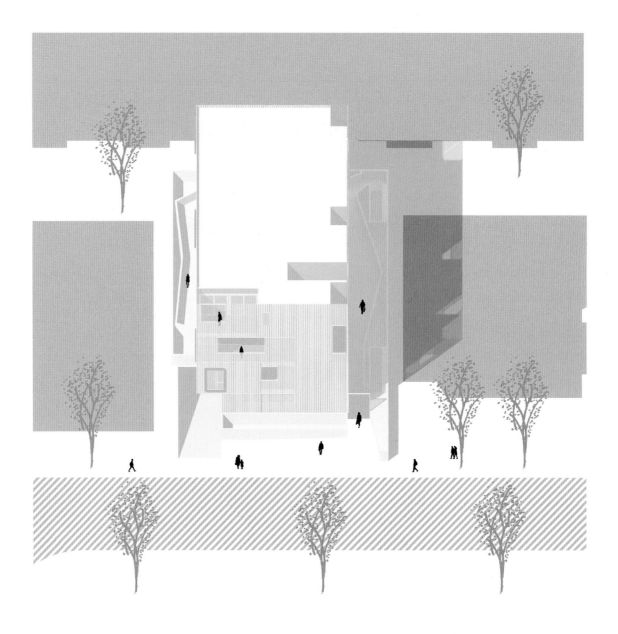

SL11024

P. 110 ←

LOCATION: Los Angeles, California
SIZE: 71,000 SF
PROGRAM: Housing and Recreational Facilities Catering to a University Community
COMPLETION: 2015
ARCHITECT: Lorcan O'Herlihy Architects [LOHA]
CLIENT: Phoenix Property Company
PHOTOGRAPHER: Iwan Baan
PRINCIPAL-IN-CHARGE: Lorcan O'Herlihy
PROJECT DIRECTOR: Donnie Schmidt
PROJECT LEAD: Abel Garcia
PROJECT TEAM: Ian Dickenson, Chris Faulhammer, Damian LeMons, Lilit Ustayan
OWNER: Phoenix Property Company

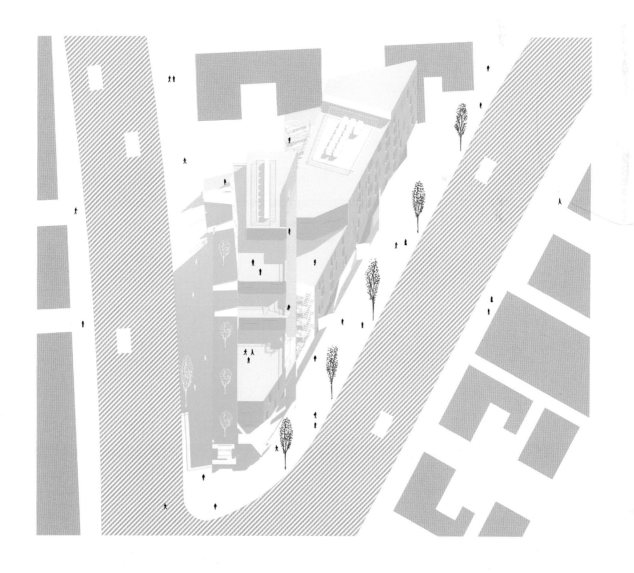

SANDI SIMON CENTER FOR DANCE AT CHAPMAN UNIVERSITY

P. 126 ←

LOCATION: Orange, California
SIZE: 72,000 SF
PROGRAM: Dance Studios, Performance Studios, Classrooms, Offices/Meeting Rooms, Lounge Spaces
COMPLETION: 2023
ARCHITECT: Lorcan O'Herlihy Architects [LOHA]
CLIENT: Chapman University
PHOTOGRAPHER: Eric Staudenmaier
PRINCIPAL-IN-CHARGE: Lorcan O'Herlihy
PROJECT DIRECTOR: Ghazal Khezri
PRINCIPAL: Ian Dickenson
PROJECT LEADS: Joe Tarr, Abel Garcia
PROJECT TEAM: Morgan Starkey, Kathryn Sonnabend
PROJECT ASSIST: Kevin Murray, Wentao Guo
OWNER: Chapman University

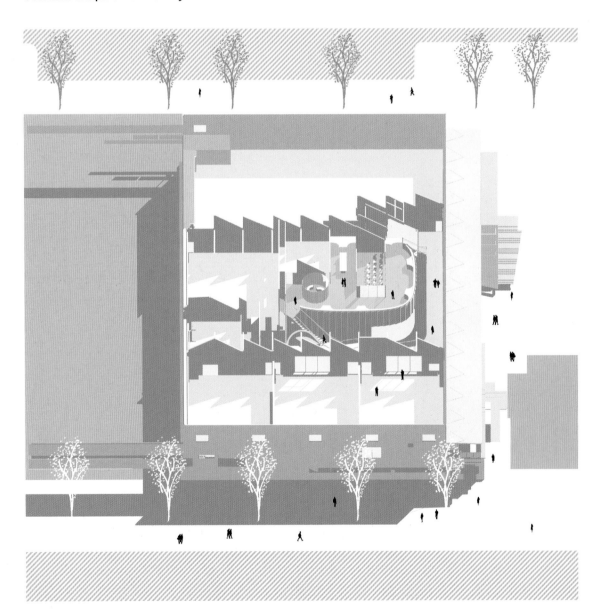

FORMOSA 1140

P. 142 ←

LOCATION: West Hollywood, California
SIZE: 28,000 SF
PROGRAM: 11-Unit Housing and a 4,600 SF Public Park
COMPLETION: 2010
ARCHITECT: Lorcan O'Herlihy Architects [LOHA]
CLIENT: Habitat Group LA, LLC
PHOTOGRAPHER: Lawrence Anderson
PRINCIPAL-IN-CHARGE: Lorcan O'Herlihy
PROJECT LEAD: Kathy Williams
PROJECT TEAM: Evan Brinkman, Kevin Tsai
OWNER: Habitat Group LA, LLC

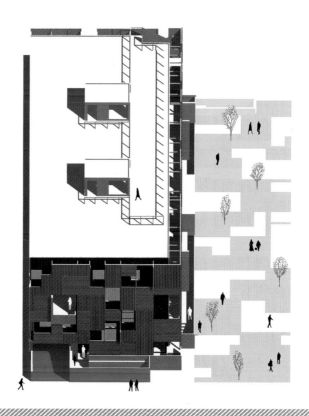

GRANVILLE 1500

P. 152 ←

LOCATION: Los Angeles, California
SIZE: 312,287 SF
PROGRAM: Mixed-Use Building with 153 Units
COMPLETION: 2021
ARCHITECT: Lorcan O'Herlihy Architects [LOHA]
CLIENT: CIM Group
PHOTOGRAPHER: Here and Now Agency
PRINCIPAL-IN-CHARGE: Lorcan O'Herlihy
PROJECT LEADS: Judson Buttner, Damian Possidente
PROJECT TEAM: Giovanni Fruttaldo, Maria Galustian,
Chris Gassaway, Rosemary Jeremy
PROJECT ASSIST: Abel Garcia
OWNER: CIM Group

WESTGATE 1515

P. 153 ←

LOCATION: Los Angeles, California
SIZE: 335,000 SF with 22,800 SF of Open Space
PROGRAM: Mixed-Use, 147-Unit Housing Project
with Street-Level Retail
COMPLETION: 2019
ARCHITECT: Lorcan O'Herlihy Architects [LOHA]
CLIENT: CIM Group
PHOTOGRAPHER: Here and Now Agency
PRINCIPAL-IN-CHARGE: Lorcan O'Herlihy
PROJECT DIRECTOR: Donnie Schmidt
PROJECT LEADS: Abel Garcia, Damian Possidente
PROJECT TEAM: Christopher Lim, Lucia Sanchez-Ramirez,
Noelle White
OWNER: CIM Group

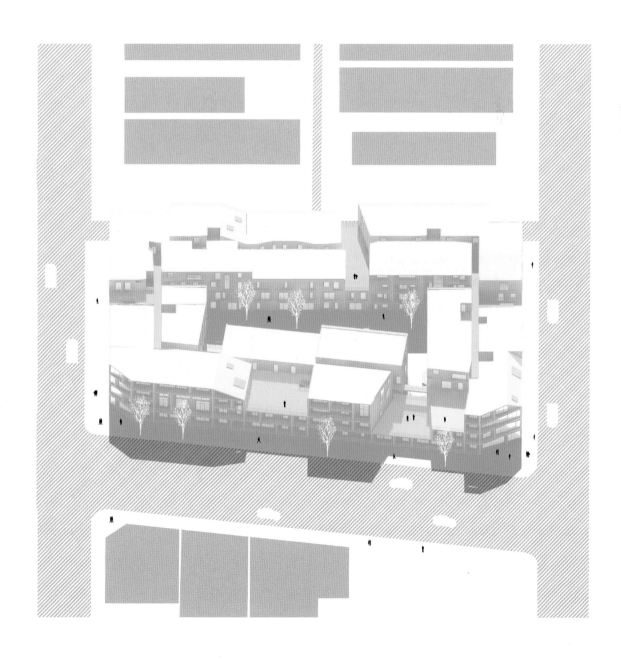

OBAMA BUILDING

P. 172 ←

LOCATION: Detroit, Michigan
SIZE: 20,000 SF
PROGRAM: Retail, Housing, and Gallery
COMPLETION: 2020
ARCHITECT: Lorcan O'Herlihy Architects [LOHA]
CLIENT: The Platform
PHOTOGRAPHER: Jason Keen
PRINCIPAL-IN-CHARGE: Lorcan O'Herlihy
PROJECT DIRECTOR: Ian Dickenson
PROJECT LEAD: Matthew Biglin
PROJECT TEAM: Benzi Rodman
OWNER: The Platform

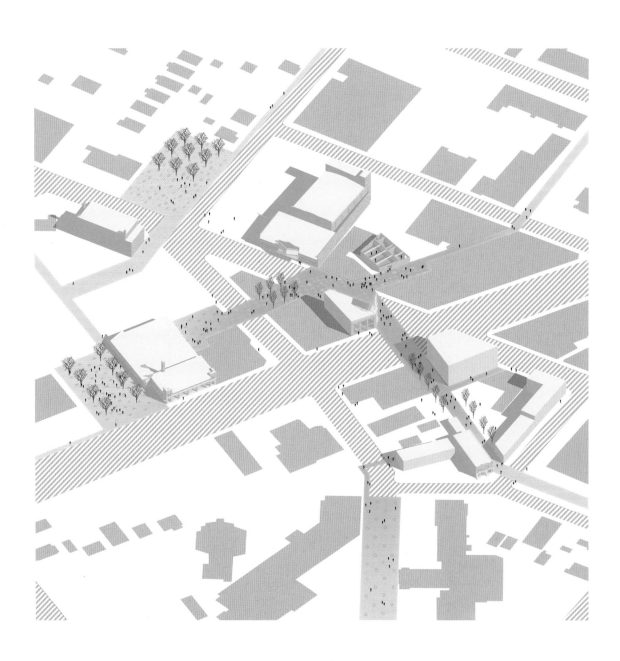

SOUTH EAST 8

P. 186 ←

LOCATION: Raleigh, North Carolina
SIZE: 5,000 SF
PROGRAM: Multi-Family Housing
COMPLETION: 2022
ARCHITECT: Lorcan O'Herlihy Architects [LOHA]
CLIENT: Merge Capital
PHOTOGRAPHER: Keith Isaacs
PRINCIPAL-IN-CHARGE: Lorcan O'Herlihy
DIRECTOR: Ian Dickenson
LEAD: Jason King
PROJECT TEAM: Kayla Manning
OWNER: Metros Capital

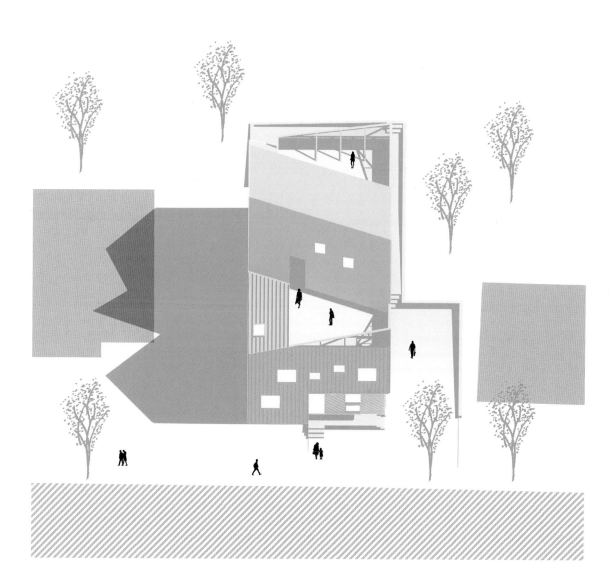

SYCAMORE 953

P. 198 ←

LOCATION: Los Angeles, California
SIZE: 64,000 SF
PROGRAM: Creative Office with Retail
COMPLETION: 2020
ARCHITECT: Lorcan O'Herlihy Architects [LOHA]
CLIENT: CIM Group
PHOTOGRAPHER: John Linden
PRINCIPAL-IN-CHARGE: Lorcan O'Herlihy
PROJECT DIRECTOR: Nick Hopson
PROJECT TEAM: Vy Drouin-Le, Abel Garcia,
Chris Gassaway, Noelle White
OWNER: CIM Group

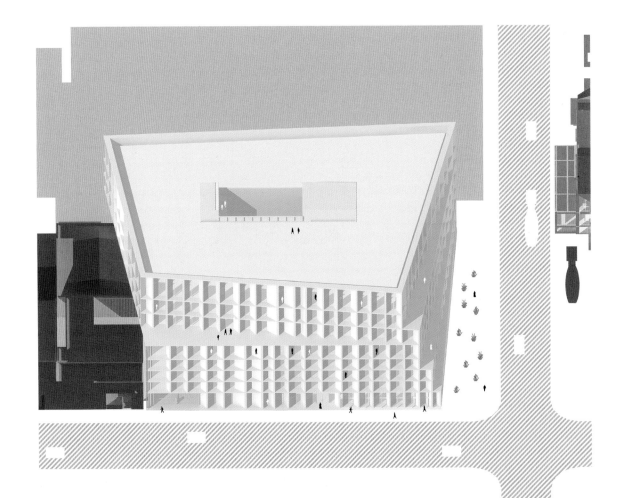

ISLA INTERSECTIONS

P. 212 ←

LOCATION: Los Angeles, California
SIZE: 34,000 SF
PROGRAM: Mixed-Use Space with 54-Unit Housing, Gardens, Creative Programming Areas, and Job Training
COMPLETION: 2024
ARCHITECT: Lorcan O'Herlihy Architects [LOHA]
CLIENT: Holos Communities
PHOTOGRAPHER: Eric Staudenmaier
PRINCIPAL-IN-CHARGE: Lorcan O'Herlihy
PROJECT LEAD: Abel Garcia
PROJECT TEAM: Ian Dickenson, Yuval Borochov, Nick Hopson, Huizhen Ng, Kathryn Sonnabend
PROJECT ASSIST: Santiago Tolosa
OWNER: Holos Communities

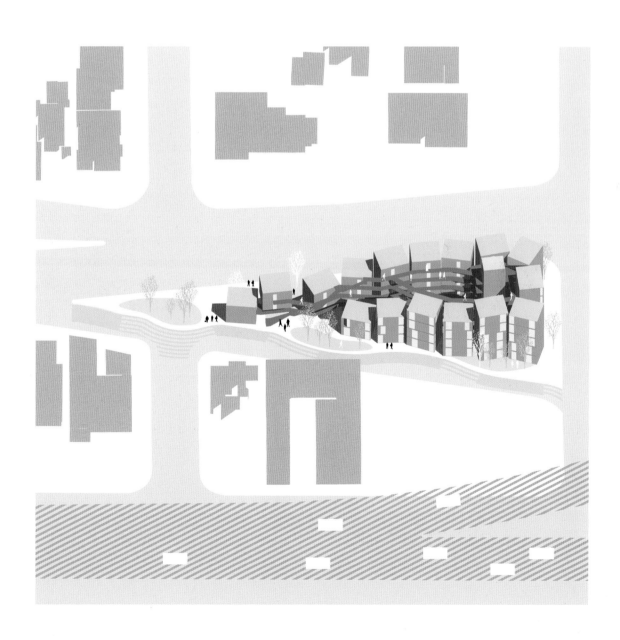

DILLON 617

P. 226 ←

LOCATION: Los Angeles, California
SIZE: 72,000 SF
PROGRAM: 49-Unit Housing
COMPLETION: 2019
ARCHITECT: Lorcan O'Herlihy Architects [LOHA]
CLIENT: CIM Group
PHOTOGRAPHER: Here and Now Agency
PRINCIPAL-IN-CHARGE: Lorcan O'Herlihy
PROJECT DIRECTOR: Nick Hopson
PROJECT LEADS: Yuval Borochov, Dana M. Lydon
PROJECT TEAM: Cameron Overy, Geoffrey Sorrell
OWNER: CIM Group

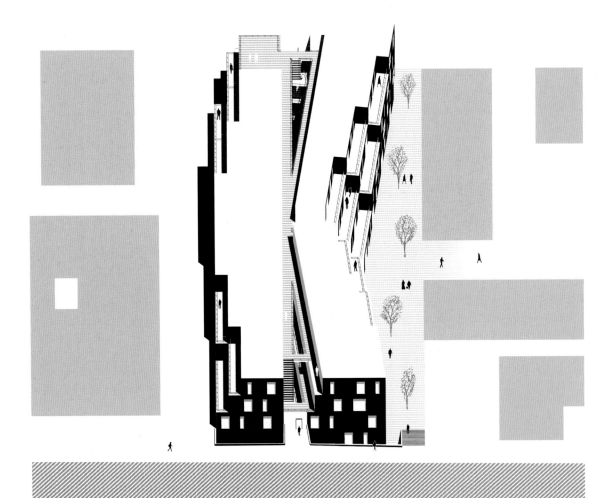

SAN VICENTE 935

P. 238 ←

LOCATION: West Hollywood, California
SIZE: 5,000 SF
PROGRAM: 7-Unit Housing
COMPLETION: 2018
ARCHITECT: Lorcan O'Herlihy Architects [LOHA]
CLIENT: Merge Capital
PHOTOGRAPHER: Keith Isaacs
PRINCIPAL-IN-CHARGE: Lorcan O'Herlihy
PROJECT LEAD: Ian Dickenson
PROJECT TEAM: Christopher Lim, Jonathan Louie, Donnie Schmidt
OWNER: 5 to 9 Group

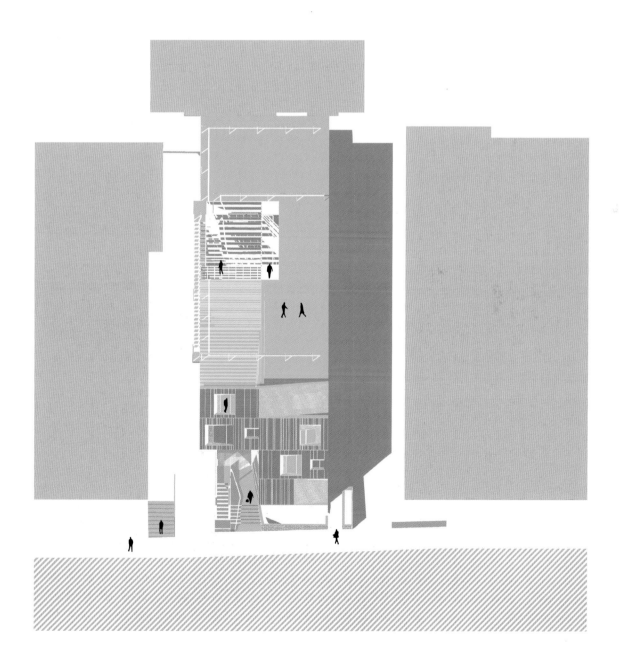

First published in the United States
of America in 2024 by
Rizzoli International Publications, Inc.
300 Park Avenue South
New York, NY 10010
www.rizzoliusa.com

For Rizzoli International Publications, Inc.

PUBLISHER:
Charles Miers

EDITOR:
Douglas Curran

PROJECT EDITOR:
Stacee Gravelle Lawrence

PRODUCTION MANAGER:
Rebecca Ambrose

MANAGING EDITOR:
Lynn Scrabis

VISIT US ONLINE:
Facebook.com/RizzoliNewYork
Twitter: @Rizzoli_Books
Instagram.com/RizzoliBooks
Youtube.com/user/RizzoliNY

2024 2025 2026 / 10 9 8 7 6 5 4 3 2 1

ISBN 978-0-8478-9952-4
Library of Congress Control Number:
2024935496

COVER PHOTOGRAPH:
Here and Now Agency

DESIGN:
Lorraine Wild and Naveen Hattis,
Green Dragon Office, Los Angeles

Typset in Lexicon designed by Bram de Does
and Hex Franklin designed by Nick Sherman.

Printed in China

MIX
Paper | Supporting
responsible forestry
FSC
www.fsc.org   FSC™ C005748